Hammer
Tacks Not Ticks

by

Dorothy Kruse

DORRANCE PUBLISHING CO., INC.
PITTSBURGH, PENNSYLVANIA 15222

Dorrance Publishing Co., Inc.
701 Smithfield Street
Pittsburgh, PA 15222
Visit our website at *www.dorrancebookstore.com*

ISBN: 978-1-4809-0872-7
eISBN: 978-1-4809-0734-8

Acknowledgements

I want to thank my good friend, Darlene Barry, for encouraging me to start writing again and my wonderful creative writing teacher, Marie Reinhardt, for sharing her talent with me.

I would also like to thank my family for providing the material for the stories. My husband, Charlie, starred in several articles and read, proofread and corrected this material over and over again. My son, Chuck, helped me with the publishing of this book.

Finally, I would especially like to thank my granddaughter, Elizabeth Kruse Hancock, for the chapter head sketches and many hours of reading and proof-reading.

Table of Contents

Introduction

One of the passions of my 81-year-old heart is writing. In grade school I wrote long, prattling letters to relatives and friends. They always said they enjoyed them, but who would tell a little kid anything to the contrary?

Later in life I entered "twenty-five words or less" contests. It was an excuse to write and a chance to win. "If I win a trip to Hollywood, I will pack Gleem toothpaste for adults in my suitcase because... when I smile, I want my gleaming white pearlies to bedazzle those big Hollywood producers into signing me to a glamorous life of show biz." My award for this was a $25 check for movie tickets.

Later on, in 1979 I wrote and sold the following jokes to a well-known comedienne. She was obsessed with her undersized breasts. Because I related to her problem, I felt qualified to contribute: "The happiest I've ever seen my husband was when a mosquito bit me in the center of my chest. He thought I'd become triple breasted. It was embarrassing. I had one big lump in the center of my chest and two smaller ones on either side."

"My husband accompanied me while I shopped for bras the other day. The clerk asked my cup size and he answered, "Demitasse!" I received $9 per joke.

A few years later, I actually sold an article. I wrote about fishing with my husband and sold it for $15. It wasn't the money that thrilled me, but the fact that someone really liked what I wrote. Charlie wasn't that excited about my newfound fame because the article titled "Big Fish Live Far Away" made fun of him. Selling that first article was the incentive and encouragement I needed to continue writing. You might even say I was "hooked."

Eventually, when our four children were in school and I had some time to myself, I joined a creative writing class. The class assignment was to produce a written piece each week. I was a full-time wife of one, mother of four, chief cook, laundress and gardener of six so that is what I knew and that was what I wrote. It worked! After using the articles as class assignments, I submitted and sold several of the same articles to newspapers and magazines. Because they were sold as first-time rights, they remain mine to resell. In the process of writing this book, I have taken those articles and inserted them back into the story of my family's life journey.

The idea for the title, *Hammer Tacks, Not Ticks*, comes from one of those articles. Attending the Annual Wood Tick Race held at the Oxbo tavern in northern Wisconsin years ago and writing about it was the impetus for some bizarre events. Yes! You read right. A wood tick race, held every first Wednesday following the opening of fishing season. It is the only wood tick race in the world and I will take you there.

Foreword

"Turn it off."

My husband Charlie and I were listening to Wisconsin Public Radio in search of smarts, not reprimands. The featured guest was a neat-nick type telling listeners, "You have too much stuff!" Before we could hit the off button, I heard, "You wear twenty percent of your wardrobe eighty percent of the time, so get rid of the eighty percent."

I'll just move it to the basement closet, I thought to myself.

"And don't just move it someplace else," hollered the mind-reader on the radio. He wasn't done. "That goes for the rest of the clutter, get rid of it!"

We had just returned from wintering in Florida and I was busy trying to stash everything we'd hauled home into already cramped spaces. In fact, that very morning I had given my annual return-from-Florida speech, proclaiming a need to sort, toss and donate, countered by Charlie's annual retort, "Yeah, yeah, yeah!"

The pesky expert on the radio was finally getting through to me. We no longer had a junk drawer, we had a junk *house*.

I started with files and files of articles and stories I had written over the years, sorting them into four boxes, one for each of our children. *I'll just sneak them into their cars when they come for a visit,* I thought to myself.

This task took me back several years when I did the same thing with family recipes. My plan was to put together a recipe book of family favorites for each of our children so they wouldn't call every time they needed a recipe.

It was a monumental job compiling and typing all the recipes on my antique Royal typewriter. When I finally finished, Charlie decided that all my hard work warranted printing more than just four cookbooks, thus *For Batter Or Wurst* came into being. Charlie, an amateur photographer, created the cover and the whole family collated and bound the collection into a recipe book. That experience was the motivation for this collection of our family's adventures and misadventures. Instead of "mm"s and "yum"s for the tummy, I hope this book provides "ooh"s and "ha ha"s for the soul.

Chapter 1

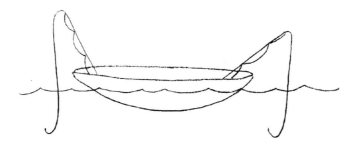

The first time I hopped across slippery, spongy bogs to the Fox River in Columbia County, Wisconsin and hooked a fish, fishing hooked me. The river was just across the road from our farm, so whenever the urge hit, I went fishing. It was fun and my catch of sun fish and bull heads were a welcome addition to our family's larder.

My equipment was a cane pole strung with heavy black line, a metal nut sinker, a cork bobber, a hook and a tin can of freshly dug worms.

I considered myself fortunate when many years later I married a man who also loved to fish, but that's when I learned there are fisher*women* and there are fisher*men*.

There were no spur-of-the-moment fishing trips with Charlie. You see, my live-in fishing partner believes big fish live far away. The first time we went fishing together, I couldn't believe he made so much work out of it – planning, packing and fussing just for a fishing trip. Thus, "Big Fish Live Far Away" became the title for my first published article, excerpted on the following pages:

Now, on a typical fishing day, we hitch up trailer and boat complete with outboard and trolling motors. We pack the car with his gear: electronic fish finder, poles, tackle boxes, minnow bucket, nets and stringer. Then my gear: fiberglass pole with monofilament line, split shot sinker, plastic bobber and night crawlers I snagged in our yard the night before. My pole has been upgraded because, according to Charlie, "that cane pole takes up too much room!"

When we finally leave, it would seem impossible to have forgotten anything, but it's incredible how many times we arrive at our destination without bait, life preserver, anchor, or some other absolute fishing necessity.

Once at the lake, our gear is moved from car to boat and we push off ready to fish, right? Wrong! We didn't drive miles and miles only to fish where we launch. Besides, I've already told you where big fish live. "Far away."

First we motor across the lake. On the way across, we meet fishermen motoring to the side of the lake where we put in. Guess where their car and trailer are parked!

When we actually start fishing, Charlie covers all possibilities. With one line he soaks a sucker. With another, artificial bait. Believe me, with all this activity, it is no easy trick to find a spot to dangle my skimpy line and crawler.

Which brings me to ask: why, when fishermen fish out of a boat, do they throw their line in close to shore and, when standing on shore, throw their line out as far as possible? Also, how come the best-selling artificial bait one season is a loser the next? Who determines the "in" lure? Fish can't talk and if they could, would they tell the truth? And who in the heck comes up with bait names like Sputterbuzz, Hula Popper, Hot 'N 'Tot, etc.? Makes me proud to be a crawler person.

I've caught most every native Wisconsin fish with my crawler-baited hook. In fact, to Charlie's astonishment and obvious envy, I have even caught a couple muskie – every fisherman's dream catch. Charlie always has an excuse or explanation – either the fish is sick or disoriented. I'd never considered the physical or mental state of a fish before Charlie. As far as I'm concerned, a fish is a fish.

I didn't get to keep either muskie. The "captain" eyeballed them and said they were too small. Of course, it is quite a different story when Charlie catches a fish. I have to hold the ruler while he stretches it for an "accurate" measurement. Would you believe it's possible to stretch a fish a full inch?

Expensive gear or not, when faced with defeat, Charlie has been known to ask me for a crawler. You can tell it pains him, but when all else fails…

From the beginning, I decided not to learn how to row the boat or operate the motor. It was an astute decision. Because my captain does all the boat handling, he has an excuse for catching fewer fish. "How can I possibly catch as many fish as she does? I spend all my time positioning her on just the right spot," he moans.

Would you mess with that? It saves my energy and his face. Actually I have a secret to catching fish, but Charlie accuses me of pulling a Tom Sawyer. We usually fish after breakfast in the morning or dinner in the evening. I do the dishes before we leave, which rids my hands of "people" scent. Charlie says he's too smart to fall for such rubbish and "no, he isn't going to do the dishes." What is a loving wife to do?

Advice to a Fisherman's Wife

"*If your hubby SHAD ask if you COD go fishing, don't be a CRAB and SHARK your duty. Go, it may keep your marriage from going on the SQUIDS. WALLEYE may have painted a CRAPPIE picture of such a trip, go for the HALIBUT, and have your self a WHALE of a time. Later, when he is giving his account of the fishing trip and you are within HERRING distance and have HADDOCK with his fish tales, keep in mind it's himself he's making a BASS of, not you. Just PERCH there and CLAM up. Let him go on with his line ABALONE. It's doubtful there's anything you could say that would make him change his TUNA anyway!*"

We are both 81 years old and still love to fish. Sometimes I wish it was as uncomplicated as when I hopped across those marsh bogs, but I'm just happy I have a live-in fishing partner and keep my mouth shut. I don't want to hurt his feelings. After all, it's one thing to hurt the one you love, but never, ever the one who paddles your boat.

Chapter 2

If it wasn't for joining a creative writing class, I'm sure I would not have devoted much time to writing. Writing would have been a "when I have time" project, but having to fulfill an assignment each week gave me incentive. I couldn't write about far away places or my life as a professional. They say write about what you know and the only thing I knew was life as a wife and mother. On the drive home after class each week, my brain would be swarming with ideas.

Because ninety percent of my time was spent with Charlie, he became the star of many of my assignments. I don't know if Charlie does things funny, or does funny things, but it was wonderful having a live-in main character.

Besides fishing, Charlie enjoyed hunting. He wanted to hunt rabbits so he bought a Beagle pup, Pokey, to be his rabbit hound. The problem was, we had a pet rabbit, so the first thing I did was teach Pokey that bunnies were "no-no"s. She was an A student. Bunny season…**CLOSED!** We also had pet turtles, but I didn't think to put them on the "no-no" list, so Pokey ate them. Well, no, not all of them. I snatched one out of her mouth just before she swallowed it.

Actually, Charlie's rabbit hound had an identity problem. She hadn't been told she was a rabbit hound. Turned out she was a bird dog. This true story was never used as an assignment for obvious reasons. I feel now, some fifty years and three residence changes later, I can finally write about it.

One day I went to go out our back door and saw Pokey standing on the top step with happy written all over her face. She was wagging her tail so hard her whole body wriggled. I asked her what she was so happy about and she sidled over to the nearby basement window, willing me to come see.

There in the window well was a whole, dressed (actually, undressed) chicken. Pokey was ecstatic with her prize. I was dumbfounded. I could only surmise the scenario: someone brought a chicken outside to grill and went back into the house for some reason. Never mind that Pokey was a rabbit dog, not a bird dog, our hunter did what hunters do – went in for the kill. We never found out where the chicken came from because we were too embarrassed to ask, and, no, we didn't have chicken for dinner that night.

Pokey's insatiable curiosity and appetite was eventually her undoing. We did not consider Pokey as we prepared for a birthday party. I don't recall whose birthday we were setting up for, but the party wasn't as joyous as it should have been. The day before the party, we hid an assortment of candy and gum on our porch. The partiers were to see who could find the most treats. The game was canceled. During the night, Pokey found the treats and ate them wrappers and all. We found her the next morning. Too much partying was her undoing. We couldn't cancel the party at such a late date, but I'm afraid none of us felt like doing much celebrating. The partiers were not told about our tragedy and somehow things went pretty well. After everyone went home was time enough to shed tears and we did.

Chapter 3

After Pokey died, Charlie decided to try his luck bird hunting. Labradors are great bird dogs, so Jenny the black lab came into our lives. Charlie was pleased with how fast his new bird dog was learning to point and fetch. Life was good. At least it was good until our daughter, Kari, brought home a wounded pigeon.

Over the years our home was home to cats, turtles, parakeets, guppies, bunnies and goldfish. The last goldfish had just recently died. We were down to Jenny the bird dog and that was the way I wanted to keep it, so it was with tears in her eyes that Kari approached me with an injured pigeon. What was I to do? You want your kids to be kind and compassionate. What a predicament!

I said the pigeon could stay until it was able to fly. It was watered, fed, coddled and named Piggy because of its appetite. First thing on the list for me: teach Charlie's bird hunter not to touch one feather on Piggy's head. Another hunting dog down!

Piggy's new home was a box on our porch. At first Piggy pecked anyone who came near her, but after a few weeks she started cooing with joy when we approached her box. That's when I decided Piggy was enjoying her convalescence a bit too much. "Take Piggy out and throw her up in the air and see if she can fly," I ordered.

And fly she did…in a sweeping, wide circle above our heads, landed in our yard, quickly waddled back to her box, and hopped in. We now had a live-in pigeon and Charlie had a damaged bird dog.

Piggy fell in love with our son, Steve. Whenever she heard his voice she'd fluff up her feathers and dance in circles. She would sit on his shoulder, kiss his face and eyes, while cooing her special love song.

She made a nest in the pen Steve built for her and laid eggs. That's when it was affirmed that "she" really was a "she." Piggy would sit on her nest until she heard Steve's voice and then hop off for a break. Steve was her chosen mate, so, playing the role, he would hold his hands over her eggs to keep them warm until she returned. Yes, I was aware that there weren't just pet problems in our household.

When the kids mowed the lawn, she would hitch a ride on the hood of the mower or the driver's head. The problem was she didn't care who was mowing. When and wherever she heard a mower, off she'd go to find her ride. I got many "come-get-your-bird" calls, but plucking a bird out of the air is almost impossible.

She was a pigeon of many interests. If I was down on my hands and knees pulling weeds in the garden, she would either prance around on my back or walk through the pulled weeds picking them up in her beak and tossing them in the air.

One day while hanging clothes on the outside clothes line, my hair in curlers, she landed on my head. I shooed her and she left with both feet trapped in a brush curler. When she circled to land, her feet still trapped in a curler, she took a nasty nose-dive.

She was multi-talented. We lived near our children's grade school so, when she heard the kids out for recess, off she'd fly to join in the fun. One year she was even given the role of a falcon in the school play.

In the other direction was a high school. Our street was the practice route for the marching band. Piggy would either circle the band overhead or march along with them.

When our daughters, Kari and Marie, lay out in the yard sunning themselves, Piggy lay on the blanket with them. If they were listening to a radio, she would dance.

She also loved to play the piano. She'd fluff her feathers, lower her head, prance up and down the keyboard and coo. One day during her concert, the door bell rang. I grabbed her and stuffed her under a skirted hassock so she wouldn't greet our visitor. It was the newspaper boy making collections, which meant I had to leave the room to get my purse. When I returned the kid was staring at the footstool with a startled look on his face. I said nothing. How do you explain a cooing hassock?

Piggy was known by people for blocks and someone apparently thought she was newsworthy because a reporter from the local newspaper called to say they had been asked to do a story about her and could they? I was scooped!

Piggy lived with us for about ten years before she died. I assume it was from old age, or maybe she was lonesome because her boyfriend, Steve, had moved out on his own. His new residence had a rigid rule against live-in pigeons.

Chapter 4

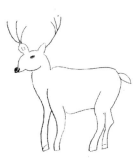

I'm grateful that dogs aren't used to hunt deer or we would have had a "deer" dog. All Charlie needed for deer hunting was a gun, license, warm clothing, and fellow card-playing, beer-drinking sharp shooters. Oh, and a wife who'd pack enough food to feed the mighty hunters and stay home and tend to household duties and kids for a week. That was me! Of course I missed Charlie, so I wrote about him.

When The Hunting Shoe's On the Other Foot

"Oh, Honey, I'm so glad to see you. I was so lonely without you this past week."

"Ditto, sweetie! Boy, I'm beat. I bet I dragged that deer a mile."

"Poor baby! But you got your deer!"

"Well, yah, but since when have you been excited about that?"

"From now on things are going to be different. Instead of resenting you for being gone for a week, I'm going to participate."

"You're going to what?"

"I'm going to participate."

"It isn't that I wouldn't want you along, but there really isn't room for another hunter in our camp, and it's all men, way out in the 'boonies,' just too rough for a woman. You wouldn't have any fun."

"Don't worry, I have no plans to intrude on you and your buddies. Besides, I've decided it is good to get away from each other and the kids once in awhile."

"Gee, sweetie, I really appreciate that."

"This brochure came in the mail the other day and it has given me a whole new outlook on hunting. You see, my participation starts after the hunt, after you get your deer. Here, take a look: Camp Cookery led by Lance Fizzeek and staff, Zack Hunck and Bart Jigalo."

"Is this some kind of a joke?"

"What do you mean? I thought you would be excited. You won't have a thing to worry about. You shoot the deer and I'll take care of the rest."

"What about the kids?"

"What do you mean?"

"I'll have to leave early from work every afternoon to pick them up from school and the minute I get home, I'll have to cook dinner. What if one of them gets sick or there's an emergency?"

"I have faith in you, honey. You shouldn't worry so much."

"But what if something happens to you way out there in the middle of nowhere? What if you get sick? What if there's a blizzard? There's no phone."

"Oh, don't get so dramatic. Everything will be just fine."

"Are you telling me that you're actually going?"

"Of course!"

"I'm not sure we can afford this right now."

"But, honey, just think of the money we'll save if I learn to process your deer. By the way, I have to go shopping tonight."

"I just got home, what's the rush?"

"Well, I have to leave the day after tomorrow, and I haven't got a thing to wear. I don't want to look like a peon and I have to pack!"

"Sweetie, I have a confession to make."

"Make it fast. I have to get going."

"I don't even like venison."

"You mean to tell me after all these years of telling us a deer would help out in grocery expenses, et cetera et cetera, and we'd like it if we'd try it, that you don't like venison?"

"Guilty! So, let's just forget this whole silly business."

"I think I know the problem. I really didn't know how to prepare venison. You're going to be so proud of me. Now come on and cooperate. Don't make me feel guilty about going. It's only for a week."

Score: Me, home run! Charlie, out!

Chapter 5

In fall of 1967, while driving down a gravel road through Wisconsin's Flambeau State Forest, we saw a "For Sale" sign at the entrance of a long, gravel driveway. As if it were staged, a beautiful white-tailed buck with a stately rack of antlers stood in the driveway. Charlie nearly lost control of the car.

Beyond that awesome buck, the land dropped off sharply so only the roof and chimney of whatever was for sale was visible. We decided to investigate and walked down the driveway to find the roof we saw from the road was covering an old log cottage. Looking in one of the windows we saw what appeared to be the kitchen with a cathedral ceiling. Hanging on the wall, in the peak of one end of the room was a beautiful antique school clock. Now I was the one who was bedazzled. As we walked around to the other side of the cottage we were treated to a spectacular view of the Flambeau River. We couldn't believe our eyes and decided then and there to find the nearest phone and call the realtor.

The cottage consisted of a large kitchen, mud room, living room, three tiny bedrooms, and, as was stated in the listing, the only bathtub in the area.

It was completely furnished: furniture, linens, pots and pans, dishes, silverware, gas refrigerator and range. The former owner was quite precise when she listed three pencils, two pads of paper in top drawer, kitchen buffet, etc." The only thing missing was a family and, after negotiating with the owners, we were happy to fill that bill. The whole transaction, a land contract, was accomplished through a local realtor, the US Postal Service and the phone. We didn't meet the sellers until many years after the cottage was paid off.

We were so excited when the whole family made the first trip to "our" cottage. It was then we found that something had been left off the list of furnishings: mice and spiders!

There was no electrical service, so no television at the end of the day. Our very first evening staying at our cottage, the kids worked on paint-by-number pictures before bedtime. Apparently the mice were attracted to them because the next morning there were little mouse footprints all over the pictures.

That was it for me. I hate mice, so the rest of that day was spent pulling out furniture and plugging any hole big enough for a pea to drop through. In spite of being told it was impossible to get rid of mice in a forest setting, we did. They still get into the cellar with an ill-fitting outside door, but I don't have to go down there.

The cottage is about a five-hour drive from home. When our four kids were young, they took turns taking a friend along so that meant we'd have seven people, our dog Jenny, clothes and food to last for a long weekend, all packed into a station wagon and car-top carrier. It was always a trip from hell: Chuck, our reader, wanted peace and quiet. Steve read every road sign aloud (not because he was interested, but because it drove everyone else nuts). Marie and Kari either sang songs - not the same one - or fought about who was looking or touching the other. Another rather strange activity they had was to spy a gray hair on their mother's head and yank it out, often without alerting me first. That activity finally lost its appeal as it became too time consuming.

The cottage was scary that first trip. The nearest neighbor is about a mile and a half away, so it is quiet. No traffic noise, no street lights, the only sounds are from an occasional owl or coyote. On a moonless, starless night, it is dark!

During the day, the cottage is an idyllic place, but there are times we can't tolerate being outside because of the pesky mosquitoes, wood ticks and/or flies. This prompted Charlie to build a small screened porch on the river side of the cottage. It juts out between two tall red pines to give us a sense of being part of the forest when we are out there. The porch is where we eat, read and just sit. It is also a great place to write; it's quiet, so there's always something worth seeing, hearing, and writing about.

It was one of those "buggy days" in the woods with the sun shining, the temperature in the eighties and a slight breeze. In fact, so slight the mosquitoes were having a field day. I couldn't stand being outside, so I was on the screened porch reading. I was so engrossed in my book, that I had become oblivious to anything or anyone. At some point I became alert and aware of the presence of a rhythmic, low-pitched sound coming from somewhere between the porch and the river.

Laying my book aside, I concentrated on where the sound was coming from. I determined it was near a tall pine about halfway between the porch and river.

As I was looking at the tree, I thought I saw a little ball drop to the ground. The mystery sound in the dense undergrowth seemed to pick up in intensity as the ball disappeared into the tall ferns at the base of the tree. Then more balls dropped. I looked up the tree trunk hoping to find the source. About fifteen feet up, I saw the wood duck nesting box Charlie had mounted a few years earlier. The little balls were falling out of that box. The balls had to be ducklings. That had to be Mom at the base of the tree, beckoning her babies to jump. The time had come to make the trek to their permanent home, the Flambeau River.

Knowing how a wood duck box is constructed, I had an idea of what the ducklings were doing inside. The box is perhaps twelve inches deep, with the entrance/exit about three-quarters of the way up. Inside the box and below the hole, Charlie had nailed hardware cloth specifically for the ducklings exit. I envisioned the awkward little fuzz balls with tiny webbed feet trying to climb that wire mesh toward the beckoning call of Mom. I wondered how many times they fell back down and had to start all over again before they made it to the exit hole.

After they got to the hole, they had to free-fall down to Mom hiding below. After living in that dark, cramped, but cozy box, the light of the outside world must have been blinding to their little eyes and terribly intimidating. Talk about a leap of faith.

I will never forget that experience and, even though the box is still used by either wood ducks or mergansers, I have never experienced their exodus again. You really do have to be in the right place at the right time.

Chapter 6

We feel so lucky to have a place where we have a bird's eye view of the Flambeau forest residents, but occasionally we experience something you would not expect to see in a forest or on a river. For instance, while you're sitting on the porch, looking down at the rippling, flowing waters of the Flambeau, would you ever expect to see a boat with armed men in military camouflage pull up along the river bank? Better yet, would you expect to see a group of identically dressed men charge out of the thick forest growth and jump into that boat? Or how about spying two burly, bearded men in plaid kilts poling the rapids on a rustic, homemade log raft heaped with camping gear?

Then there was the day our son Steve was on the river fishing when life preservers, bobbers and baits, still in boxes, came floating by. Steve thought they were gifts from heaven, but his dad and I, knowing very well he wasn't in line for heavenly gifts, decided to investigate. The mystery was solved a mile up river where we found two canoeists standing around a bonfire attempting to dry out. Their canoe had overturned, dumping them and all their gear in the process.

Another time Chuck and his friend, an avid fisherman, went fishing. Chuck could take or leave fishing, so he was the designated boat handler. He did take a pole along, but it lay in the bottom of the boat most of the time. At one point, Chuck left his lure dangling off the back of the boat, just skimming along the top of the water. Apparently, it was just what a monster muskie was looking for and Chuck had a fish. Even more remarkable, the magic lure was missing a couple of hooks. So much for stressing over what bait to use.

Then there was that sizzling, sunny July day with lots of canoes on the river. All of a sudden clouds rolled in, the wind picked up and temperatures dropped. That perfect day ended with eight freezing canoeists, in bathing suits, sitting next to a blazing fireplace in our living room drinking coffee and hot chocolate.

And, lastly, a swan song. It was only mid-September, but the closer we got to the cottage the more colorful the trees became with their fall display. It was Sunday and Charlie and I pulled into the cottage driveway just in time for the start of the Green Bay Packer football game.

We took our lunch and a radio out on the porch so that we could listen to the game while enjoying the beautiful fall day. It was during the second quarter of the game that I spied something, big, white and unusual down near the river. It slowly moved out into the open where we had a better view. "Oh my gosh," I exclaimed to Charlie. "It's a swan. Do you think you could get a picture of it?"

"I'll never make it down there in time," Charlie groaned as he bolted from his chair. He dug his camera out of the still unpacked boxes, attached the telescopic lens and hurried out the door as I sat watching the swan slowly ride by on the current. Charlie was right – he'd never make it.

He was running down the hill when all of a sudden the swan heard him, turned, and swam back to the pier. The huge, white bird seemed happy to see someone. Evidently it was accustomed to humans and most likely had been fed by them.

What do swans eat? I wondered. I immediately thought of our kids feeding ducks and geese dry bread at the park back home. I didn't have dry bread as we had just arrived at the cottage, but I had buns for the hotdogs we were going to have later. I decided I would sacrifice my bun for the cause. I ran down to the pier, bun in hand. The swan swam to meet me. I crumbled the bun and threw it into the water. It swam right by the bread and climbed out onto the muddy river's edge just below the bank where I was sitting. This wasn't a hungry swan, it was a lonesome swan.

I squatted down, eye to bill, with my new feathered friend to ask it such pertinent questions as "Where did you come from?" and "Are you lost?"

I spied a small band on its right leg and a larger one on its neck. On the yellow neck band, printed in large black letters, was "**X40.**" *That might be a clue*, I surmised.

The swan stayed around all afternoon on the river near our pier. He was dipping his long graceful neck and head underwater to eat the river plants. I was amazed how long it kept its head submerged. Charlie in the meantime was in his glory snapping away with his camera.

Checking our bird book later, we found that our visitor was a trumpeter swan. Charlie wondered if it shouldn't be in the process of migrating. Assuming Charlie was right, I figured it must be an outcast who had been ditched by his fellow swans and as a result was lost. "It's probably a male who is too embarrassed to ask directions," was my uneducated, sarcastic guess.

Just before dusk, I noticed that our feathered friend was gone, perhaps for good, but later I spied little white things floating along with the current. Upon investigation I found they were white feathers. Our friend was somewhere up river, preening and discarding its feathers. A short time later, we heard a loud trumpeting call and the swan flew down river. Had that been a farewell call?

At six the next morning, we were awakened by that same call. Our white friend was back. It again spent the day with us and in the evening, just at dusk, bedded down across the river, its long neck and head tucked under an immense wing. I wondered if it would wake us again in the morning. If so, we planned to drive to the nearest phone and call the Wisconsin Department of Natural Resources and ask if trumpeter swan number X40 was part of an experiment or study.

There was no wake-up call the next morning, nor did we see the swan that day or the last two days we were at the cottage.

Once home, I called the Wisconsin Department of Natural Resources and asked to talk to someone who might be interested in trumpeter swan X40. I was directed to call the Endangered Resource Department of the DNR, where I talked to Pat Manthey from LaCrosse, Wisconsin. She told me that she was the person who had banded number X40, a male trumpeter swan. He was part of a project to establish trumpeter swans in Wisconsin. In 1998 there were eighteen nesting pairs of trumpeters, most of them raised young. There are now about three-hundred trumpeters, fifty-one of them signets who have fledged.

According to Manthey, at least one of the some three hundred swans, number X40, has quite a reputation. In 1996, he was living on the Bad River Slough on the Bad River Indian Reservation. In the spring of 1998, he was reported to be in Babcock, Wisconsin, (about 113 miles from the cottage) before he moved to nearby Bass Lake, where he was known as an unfriendly neighbor. The residents and X40 did not get along.

If he liked you, he liked you; if he didn't, he would hiss at you, slap you with his wings, or kick you with his feet. One of the residents had a dog that couldn't go outside without being chased and hissed at by this unruly swan. Pat Manthey got so many complaints that she decided to catch the swan and move him.

He was caught, his wings clipped and given a long ride on an all-terrain vehicle to remote Swamp Lake which was only a few miles, as the crow flies, from our cottage. Once X40 molted and sprouted new feathers, he was able to fly again. Deciding he didn't like the life of a recluse, he flew back to civilization. That is when he visited us.

By the time I called Pat Manthey to report the visiting swan, she had already received word from Bass Lake saying that the ornery swan had returned and was once again up to his old tricks. The present plan was to again snag X40 and take him to central Wisconsin with the hope of giving him the urge to migrate even further south.

X40 is not welcome by people on Bass Lake, but we found him to be a delightful guest.

Chapter 7

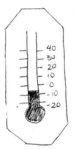

A lot of living and working took place in our lives before Charlie and I saw that buck standing in the driveway and antique clock on the wall. As a kid I felt sorry for myself because I had to work so much. At the time, I didn't appreciate the fact that hard work would actually be a great apprenticeship program for life to come. My parents' financial status was such that if I wanted or needed something, I had to pay for it. I can remember, specifically at age 15, putting a coat on layaway so I could pay for it a little at a time. I also remember making monthly payments for my first typewriter.

My first job, at about 11 years old, was babysitting. I baby sat for several families in our neighborhood. I ironed for one family and cleaned house for a couple other families. My seventh grade teacher and her husband owned an orchard and twenty-two housekeeping cottages. Every weekend, I cleaned cottages. In the fall my whole family would go to the orchard and pick grapes and apples. We made apple cider from the lesser grade apples and then sold the cider, eating apples and grapes at a roadside stand.

One family in our neighborhood had two little girls I cared for since the youngest was an infant. When I started high school, the family planned to move across town and they asked my mother if I could move with them. She gave her permission and I became their live-in babysitter.

During my senior year of high school, I only attended school in the mornings and did office work off campus until it was time to be picked up for my babysitting job. The husband of one of the people I worked for during that time was a professor who was writing a book. That summer, he hired me to type his book for him.

After I graduated, I got a full time job with the State of Wisconsin Veterans Loan Department and worked there until our first child, Chuck, was born, after which I became a stay-at-home mom – a well trained stay-at-home mom if I do say so myself.

As a young kid, Charlie collected newspapers and sold them for spending money. When Charlie was 16, his father, at the age of 47, died of a sudden heart attack. After that Charlie had to help out his mom and two sisters at home. About a year after he graduated from high school, he joined the Air National Guard and was put on active duty.

After his time in service, he began working as a clerk in a sporting goods store. That is where he was working when we got married. In ensuing years, he worked as a car salesman, ran a filling station, worked as an assistant for a furnace repairman and ran a route for a door-to-door bakery.

Delivering bakery goods paid well, but was not a good family job. Charlie left for work before dawn, got home a couple of hours before dinner and then went to bed before sunset. There wasn't much time for the kids or me, but it kept us housed and fed.

After the bakery delivery job, he signed on with a local heating and sheet metal shop as a serviceman. He earned more servicing furnaces than he had ever made before. That was because he was on call for "out-of-heat" service calls six nights a week all winter long. There were nights he didn't have any calls, but there were other nights when he'd just get back to bed and another call would come in.

In those days, most homes were heated with oil and the oil tanks were outside. When it was below zero, the oil would quit flowing. Charlie would get the call and have to lay on the snow or frozen ground and use a torch to thaw out the fuel line. When he got home and crawled back in bed, he felt like a giant icicle against my nice warm body.

Servicing those late night calls meant getting paid time and a half. Charlie can remember thinking at that time, that if he could just make $100 a week, he'd have it made for life. My, how times have changed, and this was about the time our lives really did change.

Chapter 8

One day in 1963, Charlie received a phone call from a man named Ralph Triggs. He was the owner of a local heating and cooling service shop. Ralph was a fireman who ran his service business on his free days from the fire department. He was looking for a partner and full-time employee.

Neither one of as knew Ralph. He said he called Charlie simply on the recommmendation of Frank Vultaggio, a man Charlie had worked for as an assistant repair man years earlier. Ralph explained that he needed a business partner who would be interested in purchasing half interest in his company worth $5,000. Charlie told him he didn't have $2,500. Ralph said, "I'll loan it to you!"

Charlie and I had a lot to talk about that night. We'd never heard of Ralph Triggs. Who was he? Would the two of them get along? We finally decided it was worth the chance and Charlie accepted Ralph's offer.

Ten months later, Charlie was able to repay Ralph the $2,500 and he was named President of General Heating, a company consisting of a one-and-a-half man service shop. Ralph provided what Charlie lacked in business and Charlie filled a need for Ralph as a full-time employee. They complemented each other.

At the time Charlie went with Ralph, they worked out of the basement of Ralph's home. From there they moved to office space over a tavern called The Office. How convenient. If Charlie was late coming home, he was at "the office."

Our whole family did janitorial work at General's office on weekends, or at least I did. The air there was so dry that the kids spent most of their time running and sliding in their stockinged feet so they could give each other electrical shocks.

Eventually, the company grew out of that office space and had to move. Their neighbor at the new site was a cement company. Every late afternoon the cement trucks would return to home base and rinse the leftover cement out of the carrier tanks. Charlie got the idea to use that leftover cement to make platforms for central air conditioning units General sold and installed. The company was growing.

There were so many benefits to this merger. After our son Steve graduated from high school, he joined General as a sheet metal worker. He worked there for twenty-five years before he had to retire due to degenerative disk disease.

I even came out of retirement and wrote radio ads and a company newsletter, "News in General."

As the business grew, Ralph and Charlie together took a chance on another stranger, someone who filled a growing need in their growing company. The new employee's name was Willie Chopra. Willie had both an engineering degree and a business degree, which complemented Charlie and Ralph's years of practical, hands-on experience.

By 1993, thirty years after Charlie took a chance on Ralph, General employed 120 people and they were awarded the contract to air condition the Wisconsin State Capitol building. Eventually Ralph retired and, in 1993, Charlie retired at age 62. It took Charlie a while to find his place in the workforce, but it was worth the wait. The steps he took, the people he met and the way he did business led him to Ralph Triggs and General Heating and Air Conditioning. It was a profitable, fulfilling experience.

Chapter 9

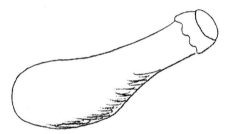

After our first child, Chuck, was born, I dropped out of the workforce. I was no longer an eight-hour-a-day employee with a fifteen-minute break in the morning and another in the afternoon. I was at least an *eighteen-an-hour-day-with-occasional-benefits* employee. Chief cook, bottle and everything else washer, child care provider, pet trainer, lawn mower, gardener were my new work titles. Of these, vegetable gardening was my favorite, which was the impetus for the following articles:

Potatoes were a must in my garden. There's nothing like the taste of little, new potatoes. So, I was delighted when I read an article about a quick and easy way to plant them. It sounded like a great time saver. All I had to do was work up the soil and lay the seed potatoes directly on the soil. No more digging a hole for them or need to cover them with soil. No hilling them when they come up and no digging at harvest time. Just cover the seed potatoes with a foot or so of seed-free mulch. To harvest, reach under the mulch and pick up as many potatoes as you want.

I did it. When the time came and I wanted a few potatoes, I reached my hand under the straw and felt around until I found potatoes. When I pulled them out, each one of my perfectly formed potatoes had nibble marks on them. By what, I didn't know. The thought of what was lurking under that mulch while I was feeling around for my spuds immediately made digging potatoes my harvesting method of choice. I would be back digging potatoes next year.

And then there's zucchini:

I love most every vegetable. Asparagus is awesome, beans are bodacious, cucumbers are cool, but by the time the Creator got to "Z" and zucchini, his creative juices had waned. Thus the zucchini, a vegetable created without self-restraint or purpose…a vegetable long in productivity and short in taste.

That was the beginning of my article, "Zap The Zucchini!" It continues:

There is nothing wrong with zucchini, but there is nothing good either. It is a taste you wouldn't miss if it were eliminated. People who can't grow anything else can grow zucchini. You never hear zucchini gardeners lament, "I planted zucchini three times and not one came up" or "I had blossoms, but no fruit."

Anyone, no matter what color their thumb, can plant a zucchini seed and successfully produce enough squash to feed an entire nation. Allot each nation just one zucchini gardener and we could feed the world. The problem is to get people to eat them. It isn't a perfect plan as people of small nations would have more squash per capita than larger nations. A rather drastic penalty for smaller nations, I'd say.

With all the excellent vegetables available, I never plant <u>zucchini</u>. I don't want to waste garden space or time to harvest and dispose of the things. I feel hypocritical trying to pretend they are delicious just to get someone to take them off my hands. In fact, recent tests have proved that zucchini is a health hazard. It causes "gardener anxiety." Begging and lying to friends and neighbors is stressful.

Oh, yes! I can just hear all you zucchini cooks exclaiming, "But you should try my zucchini bread, zucchini devil's food cake, zucchini hummingbird's tongue casserole," and on and on. People fry them in butter, smother them in tomatoes, drench them in marinade and what do they taste like? Butter, tomatoes and marinade!

I read about a masked gardener who traveled around by dark of night leaving the miserable "Z" monsters on neighbors' doorsteps. He was eventually apprehended and charged with littering and peddling an unwanted substance. Charges were dropped with the condition that the defendant never, ever plant another zucchini seed.

The only possible reason raising zucchini might be viable is if science comes up with a process to convert them into a substance for paving highways or heating homes. Better yet, how about a cure for PMS or zits? I think it behooves gardeners who insist on planting those prolific little "Z" vegetables to come up with a worthwhile function for the fruits of their labor or hang up their hoes.

Chapter 10

Gardening is labor intensive, but oh so satisfying and rewarding. I sow the seeds one day, and, even though I know there won't be any sprouts for several days, I take the daily tour to check things out. I guess it's just a case of admiring one's own handiwork.

Eventually the seeds find their way to the sun and, before long, to our tables. You can't beat freshly picked produce for good eating.

There is another great benefit to having a garden, especially for grandmas whose grandchildren come for a visit. Kids love to play in gardens. They love to play hide-and-seek in the corn and ride a big pumpkin. Gardens are harbingers of bugs and butterflies that need chasing. And what kid doesn't like to play with water? Gardens need watering. It's always a toss-up whether the plants or the kids get the wettest, but they have fun either way.

Picking a bouquet for Grandma or to take home to Mom will keep them occupied, but Grandma beware – to little ones, a flower is a flower. They are just as apt to pick your prize dahlia as they are a dandelion. "Grandma, I picked this flower just for you," is a line that can turn a loving grandma into an Oscar-winning actress in seconds. It isn't easy smiling when you feel like crying. Or how about when your sweet, above average intelligence grandchild comes to you with wide-eyed excitement and hands you the first, almost-ripe tomato – the same tomato you'd been watching so that you could pick it at the peak of ripeness. Smile, Grandma, smile!

They love to blow on a fuzzy seed-head of a dandelion and watch the white "fuzzies" swirl in the air or braid long-stemmed sweet clover blossoms into bracelets.

Writing about fun in the garden reminded me of my school days at a one-room country schoolhouse. There was a huge clump of lilac bushes in the school yard. During recess we would play hide-and-seek in the large bush mass. Over the years paths had been worn through the clump forming "rooms" for a pretend house. It was especially fun in spring when the bush was abloom with huge purple blossoms. The scent enveloped us as we made our way through the bush. It was in the 1930s when I played in that "lilac" house. I think every home we've owned since has had a lilac bush. It either came with the house or was planted after we moved in. I was moved to write the following article:

Lovely Lilacs Are Forever

If you want to do something to leave your mark on earth long after you've served your time, something that will last forever, plant a lilac bush.

One of the first things I planted when we moved into our last home was an old-fashioned purple lilac bush. My reasons: one, they are one of the earliest shrubs to bloom; two, unless someone douses it with weed killer, it will be there forever.

Early in the development of northern Wisconsin, aspiring farmers cleared land of timber so they could plant crop. Sadly, they found that the land was only good for one thing – timber. Farms failed and people moved on. Today, the sites of many of those farms are memorialized by overgrown, unkempt, but still living lilac bushes.

It is a moving sight seeing a ramshackle, gray, weather-beaten old house with a lilac bush standing at its side, a silent memorial to the family who planted it and lived there. Often it appears the house might topple if it weren't for the support of the huge lilac. If you see a single lilac bush sitting out in the middle of nowhere, just poke around and you'll likely find the rock boundaries of someone's house. The lilac out-lived the house. How many different families or generations enjoyed the sight and smell of that lilac bush? It is a melancholy thought.

Chapter 11

After moving into a house with a freestanding greenhouse, I got into gardening in a big way. Not only did I have a vegetable garden, I had multiple flower beds. I could winter things over in the greenhouse and start my own bedding plants every spring – vegetables to satisfy the appetite and flowers to soothe the soul.

Thirty some years ago, after my great-aunt Maud passed away, my dad and I had the task of going through her things to get them ready for auction. It was a sad task. As the oldest of five siblings, a few days alone at her house was the one time I really felt special. For a while, I didn't have to share things or her with anyone else. Now she was gone and all her possessions and my memories had to be dealt with.

I took my time emptying every shelf and drawer in the huge built-in dining room hutch and cabinet. Some things made me smile, some brought a tear. The feel and sight of elegant linens and the scent of furniture polish and starch all merged together. It brought back memories of special occasion dinners at her big dining room table covered with these same linens and set with her pure white Haviland china.

When I finally reached the bottom of the last drawer, I saw a sealed envelope. The rattling of the contents made me wonder if it was more bugle beads similar to what I had found in her bedroom bureau drawer.

I opened the envelope and, instead, there were seeds. I couldn't identify them, so I slipped them into my pocket. There was one way I could find out what they were and that was to plant them and wait for them to grow. It was possible they were too old and dried to sprout, but I wanted to give them a try.

At home, every inch of garden space had already been planted, but I needed to find room for my seeds. We had just converted from oil to gas heat in the greenhouse and gotten rid of the outside oil tank in back of the building. As I worked the soil, I could smell the odor of fuel oil. It must have leaked from the tank over the years, but without another spot to plant the seeds, I decided to chance it.

I was thrilled when a couple of weeks later I saw the first tiny sprouts, but I couldn't identify them. As they matured, the leaves became velvety and bluish green in color.

It was fun watching them grow, and grow they did into lush bushes about three feet tall. The leaves were bigger than my hand. One day I noticed long white buds had formed. In about a week, the buds opened into pure white trumpets and had a wonderful, delicate, sweet scent. The buds waited for late afternoon shade or early evening to unfurl their long white blossoms. I knew as soon as I saw them they were moonflowers, why, I don't know, because I don't ever remember seeing them before. I got out my seed catalog to check and there they were, moonflowers.

I considered it a final gift from Auntie and I bet she had a smile on her face as she saw my delight and surprise. They were surely mystery seeds.

In the fall, after the plants stopped blooming, round, prickly seed pods formed. They eventually dropped onto the ground where I left them to dry. At some point they split open and emptied their seeds, the same seeds that were in the envelope from Auntie's buffet drawer. Every spring they sprouted on their own.

When we moved, I took some pods with me. I didn't want to lose my moonflowers and my special connection with Auntie, but the connection was broken. The seeds didn't sprout at our new home. I tried everything, planting them indoors in pots, strewing the seeds on the soil in the fall, but nothing worked. Was it Auntie encouraging me to move on and not put so much importance on things in the past? Could be. She was a wise lady who made a big impact on my life and feels she still has more to do.

Chapter 12

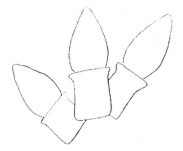

"We don't have much money, but we sure have a lot of fun" was Charlie's motto. He loved riling me and our neighbor ladies by telling us how good we had it staying home every day watching soap operas and napping while our husbands were wearing their fingers to the bone trying to support us.

When I was in the hospital giving birth to our fourth and last child, Marie, Charlie took a few days off to stay with our three other children. The first morning, he got up early, fed the kids, did the dishes, made the beds, picked up the house and put a pan of refrigerated cinnamon rolls to bake in the oven. At 8:30 AM, he called the neighbor ladies inviting them over for coffee. "I have all my work done and feel like taking a break," he told them.

They all turned him down saying they were too busy. The next morning, while he was reading the paper, the house in shambles, kids still in pajamas and beds unmade, they all appeared at the front door wanting to join him in a coffee break.

They got him, but didn't disable him. The day after I got home from the hospital, I went to the grocery store. Baby Marie was sleeping and Charlie was babysitting. A neighbor called to see if Charlie and I could join them for a cup of coffee. It was a beautiful warm July day and they wanted us to bring the new baby down so they could see her. He told them I was gone and he was babysitting, but thanks anyway.

He knew if the neighbors were having coffee, they were sitting at their kitchen table looking out the large picture window towards our house. It was showtime! He took our oldest daughter's life-sized doll and bundled it up in a baby blanket and started toward the neighbors. They could see him coming. He got halfway there when he suddenly tripped, throwing his precious bundle up in the air and watched the neighbors lift up off their chairs, their hands flying up to their terror-filled faces. As they watched him pick up his decoy baby, they realized they'd been had again. One of the neighbor women said that she knew for sure he took ten years off her life.

It wasn't often he got a little of his own medicine, but our oldest daughter Kari and I managed to do a pretty good job one late November. Charlie decided to test the bulbs on our outdoor Christmas lights and get them up before it snowed. He carried his box of lights out on the driveway where he had room to string them out and see if they worked. The first string had several dead bulbs, so he decided to run into town and buy replacement bulbs. While he was gone, Kari called to say she was stopping over. I warned her about the lights on the driveway. She arrived before her dad returned and stopped before she got to the lights. While we were visiting, I was looking out the front window at her car and our Christmas lights and realized we had the makings of a great prank. It was time to get Dad for a change.

Kari went outside and, lying on her stomach on the cold driveway, she threaded the string of lights under her car. She then took the cardboard box, emptied out the contents and scrunched it under her back tire. We were so pleased with ourselves. It was agony waiting for Mr. Prankster to return.

We watched as he approached. He pulled into the driveway and suddenly slammed on the brakes. His hands flew up to his forehead and he just sat in the car, shaking his head back and forth in disbelief. He looked completely defeated as he finally got out of the car, his now useless replacement bulbs in hand. When he stepped inside the house and saw Kari and I waiting for him, he realized that the joke was on him. It was April Fool's Day in November.

Chapter 13

During my teenage babysitting jobs, I was sure when I got married I would have at least a dozen kids. I loved taking care of them. It just took my first baby to make me back off on that dream. Our first baby, Chuck, had colic for the first three months of his life. That was not fun. There were no parents coming home, thanking me and paying me for baby sitting, and then walking me home to my own quiet, peaceful bedroom. I was a *mother*!

I think I was a pretty good mom. I sure was a busy one. Our four children were about two years apart in age. Now when I think back to the time when I had a new baby, plus a two-year-old, a four-year-old, and a six-year-old, I wonder how I managed. I guess it is just that you do what you do when you have to do it.

Of all the motherly duties, teaching our kids to drive was one of my least favorite. Charlie helped out when he could, but he worked during the day and I was a stay-at-home mom.

Being a driving instructor was especially hard for me because I don't like to drive. I didn't get my license until I was nine months pregnant with our third child, Steve. I think the guy that was assigned to me passed me out of sympathy and didn't want me to return. My belly was so big I could hardly reach the steering wheel.

Eventually all four kids had their licenses, but that didn't mean I had peace of mind. A teenager's idea of what getting a driver's license means and what a parent figures they're qualified for are *miles* apart. To prove my point, I wrote the following article:

Once Around the Block

"Mom, can I use the car tonight?"
"Sure, but just once around the block."
"Motherrrrr!"
"Okay, twice, but that's it."
Our youngest daughter, Marie, had just gotten her driver's license a week earlier. I still couldn't believe she passed on the first try.

When they called her name to take the behind-the-wheel test, she couldn't find the car keys. She lost them while we were waiting in the reception area. I was silently delighted. Surely such irresponsibility would be taken into consideration.

I knew my prayers had gone unanswered as soon as she returned. She came bouncing back to me, with a big smile and announced, "I passed!" History had repeated itself. Just like my experience years earlier, they didn't want her back.

A week after Marie got her license, our oldest daughter Kari called and asked Marie if she could do her a favor. Kari's dog was sick and needed to go to the vet and Kari wasn't able to do it. Marie was free, so she agreed to help her out.

As usual, Marie had to take a girlfriend along. Teenagers can't do anything by themselves. So the two girls and the dog, which insisted on sitting on Marie's lap, took off for the vet's office.

On the way, Marie felt her lap getting warm. She instinctively rose up off the seat, trying to get the dog to move so she could see what was going on. It didn't take long to find out. The dog was depositing some of his discomfort on Marie's lap, which rolled onto the seat beneath her. She didn't want to sit back down and the dog wasn't finished. Marie yelled to her friend to hold on to the steering wheel, while she rolled down the car window and held the dog's rear out the opening.

All this was being accomplished while they drove through a twenty-five-mile-an-hour speed zone at about fifty or so. Because, she explained later, "when I rose up out of the seat, my weight was on the foot which was on the gas pedal." Certainly anyone could understand that, but why, I wondered, didn't she pull off to the side of the street and stop? The answer was simple. "Motherrr, everything happened so fast, I just didn't think." Now that I believe.

Pictures of our car speeding down the street, a dog's rear hanging out the window and the passenger steering flashed in and out of my mind for days. It would wake me from a sound sleep. Now she wants to go to a dance. At night. Oh, well, at least when it's dark, there will be less chance anyone will recognize our car and who, or if anyone, is steering.

You know, it may not appear that way, but I have been trying to have some small sense of continuity in this book, so I'm wondering if this is the place I should mention that our oldest son, Chuck, graduated magna cum laude? Oh, well, this is as good a time as any.

Chapter 14

Having to come up with a written piece every week for my writing class can be a challenge. I don't mind writing about Charlie's shortcomings, but when I have to write about mine, you know I'm grasping.

I've already told you that I do not like to drive. Charlie does ninety-five percent of the driving. I write when I'm in the car. The title of this assignment/article is WIMPS, Women Immobilized by Motorcar Phobias, which was written in the car:

WIMPS is a support group for women with driving disorders. We have members in fifty states. At present, we are not accepting additional members as it has become progressively difficult to cope with the needs of the current membership and their diverse problems. In this article, I will try to outline those problems, hoping to give you a better understanding of WIMPS and the many disorders we deal with. Our president and founder suffers from the fear of merging, sometimes driving as much as thirty to forty miles out of her way to avoid having to do so.

She is a very stable person in every other way, never looking over her shoulder, always looking ahead, which some say may be part of her problem.

Another member cannot back up. She's the one that always pulls through parking stalls so that she is faced out when she leaves, thus driving against parking lot arrows. Her sympathetic, understanding husband backs her car into their garage every evening when she arrives home from work so that she'll be headed in the right direction the next morning. One evening he forgot and it resulted in several thousands of dollars of damage to their home. Actually, it wasn't the end of the world. With front and back garage doors, he no longer has to worry about which way her car is headed.

One of our newer members can't turn left. This isn't quite so problematic, because she found if she takes enough right turns, she'll eventually arrive at her destination. Granted it might take longer, but she adjusts.

This hasn't been a problem during her entire driving life. She noticed it at the age of forty after she had her appendix removed. Since that time she has favored her right side and even lists some in that direction.

Our president, who cannot merge, is a little more vague about when she first noticed her phobia, but she feels it was about the time she got married and does not care to go into details.

The most troublesome problem presented to WIMPS was the woman who was afraid to drive over water. This woman lives, of all places, in the Florida Keys. When she first joined the club, she said she had to close her eyes every time she approached a bridge. She scraped the passenger side of her car along the outer edge to get across. If you've ever driven on one of those Florida bridges, you know your tires make a horrible racket so she was aware when she came to the end of the bridge.

She understands this isn't a safe or reasonable approach to her problem and came to WIMPS for help. What is particularly bothersome is that she is driving on drawbridges. She's afraid if she has her eyes closed and the scraping noise stops, the next sound she'll hear is a loud splash.

At this time, our membership is closed so that we can work out the following administrative problems:

First of all, there is the problem of a meeting place. As the membership has become more widespread and the problems have become more diverse, we have found it exceedingly difficult to assemble. At this time, we connect by cell phone from our own homes at a designated time and serve ourselves dessert and coffee. This is not productive. In fact, it is creating another problem…obesity. We're now in the process of starting a weight loss group, WOW, for Women Over Weight. The End (I hope), Dorothy Kruse, President

The truth be known, WIMPS hasn't done a thing for me. I still don't like to drive. Charlie will just have to keep on driving while I keep on writing. And there's a lot of stuff to write about when you're mindlessly riding along. Either I make something up or I see something worth noting. For instance, messages on billboards or church signs. A United Methodist Church sign I saw read, "'Don't make me come down there!' signed God." Another message from God: "Will the road you're on get you to my place?" A Catholic church displayed a sign that said, "A tongue isn't very heavy, but some people find it hard to hold." That was a favorite of Charlie's for some reason.

The car radio can also be informative and touching. This is a line from a country-western song I heard, "He's going to drive a truck in heaven 'cause he's a truck drivin' man." I'm telling you, that nearly ate my heart out.

I was also informed by listening to the radio that an in-depth survey by the Farmers' Almanac found that, "Weirdness is up forty-four and a half percent." Now how in the heck did they calculate that? If it's in the Farmers' Almanac, it must be so. I wasn't even polled.

While driving through Southern Georgia on our way to Florida, I listened to a radio swap shop. A listener called in with "two billy goats and some big ole dogs for sale." This swap shop was sponsored by Dad's Café where, "Southern Cookin' makes you good lookin'." I tried to get Charlie to stop, but when he's a go'n, he ain't a stop'n!

There are a couple of business signs in Florida that are favorites of mine. A second-hand furniture store advertises: "Pre-Loved Furniture." A pest control sign reads: "Nite-Nite Termite." My favorite sign is displayed at a car dealership: "I'd Give 'Em Away, But My Wife Won't Let Me." Again, the wife gets the blame. Once we get to Florida, we listen to a radio station that features the golden oldies. Their slogan is, "If you can't hum 'um, we don't play 'um." On the same station, a car dealership promises, "We'll give you a deal you can brag about." That's what I'm looking for.

Chapter 15

Wₑ're on our way home from the cottage. The signs along the road for the next five hours are signs I've seen for years, so nothing to write about there. I'm not even looking for something to write about – I have something to write about. In fact, the something I have to write about was the impetus for the title of this book. While we were in the North Woods, we went to a wood tick race. That's right, a wood tick race, and I couldn't quit thinking about it.

The annual Wood Tick Race is held every first Wednesday after the opening of fishing season at the Oxbo Tavern in Oxbo, Wisconsin. This is the largest social event in the area, an area where the only social venues are bars such as Nine Mile, Six Mile, and Three Mile Taverns. The names denote the distance to the closest town, Fifield, Wisconsin. The Oxbo Resort is at the end of the line-up of taverns along Wisconsin Highway 70 on an oxbow-shaped bend in the Flambeau River.

When we first heard about it, we figured it had to be a joke, but there is not a lot going on in the North Woods, so we decided to check it out. When we arrived we were lucky to find a parking place. We got out of the car and with all the noise coming out of the place there had to be something going on, and there was. People were standing around a pool table yelling and cheering, greenbacks in their hands, focusing on two wood ticks sitting on a bull's eye target in the center of the pool table. The ticks had names: Garfield, Satchal, Slowbutt, and Trickie Dickie (may give you a hint as to who was President of the United States at the time). The first tick out of the bull's eye was the winner. The other one was the loser and was smashed with a hammer by the Head Tick Master. This went on until there was only one tick left and he/she was declared the winner. The tick's owner was awarded a trophy to be displayed at the Oxbo Tavern.

So, that was what I was thinking about on our car trip home, back to sanity. I just knew there was a story there somewhere. I got to thinking about all the "societies" for the prevention of this that or something else and wondered, *What about the poor wood tick?* Thus the following letter to the editor of the *Sawyer County Gazette* (where the race took place):

As President of SPHLATS (Society for the Prevention of Hammering Less Agile Ticks), I feel it my duty to issue a protest against the annual Oxbo Wood Tick Race. Ticks are caught and kept in stinky matchboxes, cans, jars, and bottles (some of them unwashed) until race time. During the race, ticks are prodded with assorted objects and subjected to abusive language spewed upon them by liquor-laden breath. If a tick isn't agile enough to win, it meets death under the hammer.

We, the members of SPHLATS, have taken time to get to know these affectionate creatures who so eagerly attach themselves to us. They are without prejudice whether it be sex, religion, color, or political preference. They treat each of us equally: rich, poor, ugly, or beautiful. Their interest is only in our inner selves.

Ticks make wonderful pets. They don't require special housing, litter box, or change of paper each day. They are even content to share our beds.

We aim to see that the wood tick does not become the next endangered species. SPHLATS motto is "Hammer Tacks, Not Ticks."

If you are as "ticked off" as I am and want to see these hammerers nailed and sent to the slammer and, more importantly, want every cruel, inhumane wood tick race in the world shut down, write to us. We need your support. A "Keep Ticks Intact Kit" will be sent to you for a nominal fee. For more information the address is...

There was no response after the letter appeared in the local newspaper. Readers in the North Woods just chalked it up to another nutty "city" person. It wasn't until *The Milwaukee Journal* (now *Milwaukee Journal Sentinel*) picked it up and published it that I got letters. They were requesting the non-existent kits. The requests weren't just penciled notes on yellow-lined tablet paper. One request was on Alaska Department of Health and Human Services letterhead.

I felt obligated to respond, but without kits, I decided to send out feelers to measure the sincerity of the requests. Plus, I had to have money to produce them. I was positive once they were told they had to pay for such nonsense, interest would wane and my problem would be solved. I wrote:

We at SPHLATS were very pleased to hear from you and are happy to send you the following information about our Keep Ticks Intact Kit.
Kits will include;

1. *Membership certificate suitable for framing.*
2. *Device for removing wood ticks in a humane manner, plus instructions.*
3. *Bumper sticker with SPHLATS slogan "Hammer Tacks, Not Ticks."*
4. *Wood tick game.*
5. *Wallet-size membership card.*
6. *Live wood tick sent upon request.*

The cost of the kit is $3.50. We hope to hear from you soon. In the meantime, remember: all wood tick lovers "tick together."

Tick lovers are not cheap; they wanted kits. Everyone sent a check. And would you believe, some even wanted the optional *wood tick*. Now, not only did I have to produce kits, I had to hunt down wood ticks.

The tick-removing device was a bird feather with instructions to tickle the ticks until they laughed so hard they let go. (It was easy finding molted bird feathers lying around.) I made up "Hammer Tacks, Not Ticks" bumper stickers. "I'll Find Your Tick, You Find Mine" was the game with the explanation that there are places on a person's body that are impossible to inspect personally, so you engage a partner of your choice to help. Individual taste would dictate the degree of fun. I designed kit materials, took them to the local print shop (this was during pre-computer days), assembled kits, and mailed them out. My cost estimate was off, so I went into the hole financially, as well as with Charlie, but it was done.

My relief was short-lived. I found out just how successful word-of-mouth advertising can be. More requests came in. On my first trip to the printer, I only printed kits to fill requests in hand. Thankfully I saved the master, because I ended up making several more trips. Every time I sent out a batch, new requests came in.

Eventually they stopped, much to my relief, as each order put me deeper in debt. But Oxbo tick racers wanted more so I wrote a novelette, *The Tale of the Tock Ticks*, about a tick family named Tock. The big mystery in their lives was the disappearance of Cousin Tilford who dropped out of sight one first Wednesday after the opening of fishing season. This too was reprinted several times and, again, at a loss. A businesswoman I'm not, but I learned several things: one, that people are hungry for fun and laughs. Two, I don't know a darn thing about estimating the cost of producing or publishing printed matter. And finally, that there actually are people who loved ticks. By the way, the Wood Tick Race is still an annual event.

Chapter 16

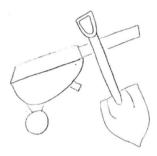

I really missed the old "twenty-five words or less" contests after they disappeared from the scene, so I was very interested when I heard about a writing contest sponsored by Garrison Keillor. Charlie and I listen to Garrison Keillor's weekly show on our local National Public Radio station, WHA. His challenge was to write "Why you think your town is the real Lake Wobegon," the town Garrison features on his show. The prize was tickets to Garrison's live appearance at a local theater. I decided to use excerpts from articles I had previously written along with lines and characters from Garrison's show. The following is the result:

> As I peer past the Kestol's big blue Harvestore at the blue-green waters, amid marsh grasses, I know I'm in real Lake Wobegon. Our women are strong, as strong as the coffee they brew. Our men good lookin', if you put emphasis on the inner self, and our children above average – they're smart enough to leave as soon as they're eighteen.
>
> When you see "Welcome" and "Come Again" on the same sign, you know you've been here. The sign stands in the town triangle (there wasn't enough room for a square) midst a bed of pansies. Cora Ledbottom plants the pansies every spring. She also models for the popular bent-over lady lawn ornament with the frilly panties.

There aren't a lot of differences between Lake Wobegon and bigger cities; things are just done on a smaller scale. For instance, roadwork is done with a wheelbarrow and shovel. When we go to the town hall for a meetin', we can also buy groceries, belly up to the bar, play a game of pool, have a pizza, and buy fish bait. We're the originators of one-stop-shopping.

Lake Wobegon is a quiet, private town, so we don't encourage anything touristy. The only major event is the annual wood tick race, a fundraiser for the Lutheran Church.

Crime is nearly non-existent. There's only been one arrest in Lake Wobegon history. It was a tough crime to crack, but the criminal finally did herself in. Zucchini squash was mysteriously appearing on doorsteps along with recipes for Zucchini Devil's Food Cake, Zucchini Bread, Zucchini Stir-fry, etc. At first people thought it was a kind deed, but it got to be a nuisance. Someone finally called the sheriff, citing trespassing and littering as the charge. The sheriff was stumped until the day of the Luther Leaguer's annual potluck when, lo and behold, someone brought a zucchini marshmallow salad. Lidia Peakem looked on the bottom of the dish and there on a piece of adhesive tape was the name Sara Skulk. The sheriff arrested Sara, who got off on an insanity plea: stress due to zucchini over-production, plus a promise never, ever to plant another zucchini seed as long as she lived.

Probably the most notorious citizen of our town is Clyde Craft. His idea revolutionized calf farming in the Lake Wobegon area. Clyde's plan was to take a giant hay bale, cut out the center and shove a calf in the cutout. The bale would serve as both shelter and food. He called them Hay Hutches. When the bale was gone, the calf was ready for market. The hay centers were sold as hay hearts to city slickers for mulch.

This was a boon to our town because when our farmers are happy and prosperous, so are we in Lake Wobegon.

Charlie and I attended the Garrison Keillor show with our free tickets!

Chapter 17

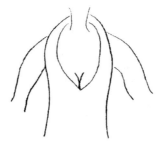

If I want a really ridiculous and funny story, I usually have to make it up, but then there are times fact is as good or better than fiction. Charlie proved that without even trying. It happened one very hot July day at the annual Art Fair on the Square in Madison, Wisconsin. As usual, art lovers were shoulder to shoulder, some pushing baby strollers and others leading their "I-just-can't-be-without-them" canines.

This popular event draws people from all over the United States. The displays and artistic creations are spectacular. It is no easy trick to view the merchandise, not step on a dog's tail or foot and keep track of your partner all at the same time. Several times I gave an unsolicited commentary on an article to a disinterested and bewildered stranger.

One particular booth displayed leather items: purses, belts, vests, and skimpy halters. Two well-endowed models made the halters look even skimpier. However, there was a leather purse in the booth that caught my eye and I wanted to point it out to Charlie. Having learned my lesson earlier, I looked before I spoke, making sure it was Charlie's ear I was talking into. I'm glad I did, because my Charlie was not beside me. In fact, my Charlie was several feet away and he had found someone new. His hands were on her shoulders, pulling her back against his chest while, with a devilish grin on his face, he was either nibbling her ear, or whispering something into it. Whatever he was doing, it wasn't working. The poor woman's eyes were filled with horror. At the moment I saw him, he saw me and panic filled his face. He let go of his new lady so abruptly she nearly fell to the sidewalk.

As we hurriedly left for our car, my unfaithful husband explained that I had been in front of him just seconds earlier and he thought it would be funny if he whispered in my ear, "Would you like a leather bra?"

By the look on the lady's face, she either didn't take gifts from strangers or she didn't like leather bras. I'm thinking Charlie was extremely fortunate he wasn't arrested. The lesson of the day: take time to know your audience!

Because the Art Fair on the Square is such an important event, I wrote up the incident and submitted it to one of our local newspapers, the newspaper to which we subscribe. After I got notice that the article was accepted, I thought I should warn Charlie that it would be appearing soon. As a local business owner who did his own radio ads using his real name, he'd become fairly well-known in the area, which prompted him to ask, "You didn't use my name, did you?"

I was happy to tell him that indeed I hadn't used his name, but the paper always gives credit to the author of an article and her name is Dorothy Kruse.

Chapter 18

I suppose it would only be fair, if I write about a Charlie fiasco, I should do the same for me, although I really had to look long and hard before I found something.

This involves our youngest daughter, Marie, who by this time was married and had a baby son. She was working for a student loan collection agency. Her employer was sending her to Los Angeles to appear in a court case. At that time, Marie had never flown or traveled anywhere on her own. I, her well-traveled, sophisticated mother, on the other hand was travel savvy???

I was nervous about her trip to the big city of Los Angeles and drove her crazy with new advice every day. My first and most important rule was to be sure to remember the name and address of her motel/hotel so that she would be able to get back there after the court hearing.

I lay awake every night making up disastrous scenarios until I talked myself into going with her. By waiting until the last minute, the cost of a ticket was staggering, but it was Mother to the rescue.

We left Madison's airport and flew into Chicago's O'Hare field. Following is the chain of events for my daughter and her travel guide mother:

1. Arrived at O'Hare, found that our flight to L.A. was delayed an hour and a half.
2. Arrived in Los Angeles, Marie was paged as we waited for our luggage. Case was settled out of court. We could go home.
3. Collected luggage, walked about a mile to exchange return tickets for next day.
4. Took shuttle to motel where Marie's boss had made reservations.
5. Found our motel was in a seedy neighborhood. If we were interested in a tattoo or massage, we were in the right place. The lobby was the size of a large phone booth and had bulletproof glass and bars on the special "night" window.
6. Room clean, but window, which was off the third floor outdoor walkway, had a broken lock. Pry marks on the window frame were evidence that someone had forcibly tried to remove the screen that, as a result, was bent and ill fitting.
7. Had to eat, but no restaurant in the motel. Called the local lawyer connected to the case. He suggested the restaurant at the Hilton near the airport.
8. Cab driver warns us not to go out alone after dark and gave us his number so we could have him take us back to our motel when we finished eating.
9. Had a wonderful meal. A harpist in pink chiffon was undaunted by all the clinkers she struck as she serenaded the diners. For additional entertainment, there was a rather unsavory looking man with two scantily dressed ladies in a booth next to us. I assumed it was a business dinner. Bits of conversation such as "my girls" from the man and "thought it was a good area near the airport" from the girls gave hints as to what kind of business they were discussing.
10. Finished dinner, called our cab driver for return trip. He was unavailable.
11. Realized we were so assured of his promise to take us back to our motel, we didn't have the address. (Veteran traveler, Mom's number one rule of things not to do.) We knew it was a Best Western, and that it included the word "airport," but according to the doorman there were two possibilities. We came up with a partial spelling of the street so with some brainstorming by a limo driver, doorman, the man in charge of valet parking and a man who just seemed to be hanging around, they thought they knew where we belonged. The doorman said he'd have a cab up right away. A Cadillac pulled up, the doorman opened the backdoor, and we got in. Once inside, it dawned on us, not only wasn't there a cab company printed on the sides of the vehicle, but there was no meter. To make it worse, the driver was the man who appeared to be loitering near the hotel entrance. We were

just a little more than a bit anxious about the position we were in. The driver asked how much it cost us to get to the Hilton. We told him $7.50, whereupon he assured us he knew where to deliver us. And he did! I don't know who or what he was, but we were more than grateful to arrive back to our "sleazy" motel.

12. I took a shower. Water just barely warm.

13. Went to bed, fell asleep only to waken and find Marie still awake and scared.

14. I asked if she would like to sleep with me as my bed was further away from the door and window. Yes, she would and did, but before she changed beds we wedged a folded luggage stand into the window so that no one could push it open.

15. Shortly after midnight, we were startled by a loud thumping by our door. For some reason, we both jumped out of bed and ran to the door. What we planned to do, I'm not sure. Finally determined that someone was having trouble getting into the room next door to us.

16. Slept with TV on the rest of the night.

17. In morning, Marie took a shower figuring it would be lukewarm like the night before and almost scalded herself.

18. Got free coffee, donuts, and L.A. Times from lobby.

19. On way back to our room, Marie spilled coffee on back of my jacket and slacks.

20. Took photos of motel and surrounding area. We were sure no one would believe that there was a beat-up car sitting in the courtyard next to the empty pool.

21. Time to go to the airport. I leave the room first. A couple of muscular, shirtless beach boys were repairing the door of the room next to ours. Probably the same door someone was pounding on the night before. They didn't move an inch as I struggled by with my purse, book, coat and suitcase. Marie breezes out with a small overnight case and purse and both men dropped their tools and asked if she needed help.

22. Took shuttle to airport. When unloading our things, I notice Marie's necklace on the floor of the shuttle. She had no idea how it got there. We think she dropped it the day we arrived and it was still there.

23. We're told our flight home had been canceled.

24. Stood in line to reschedule. Man in back of me taps my shoulder and pointed to a sock on the floor asking if it belonged to me. Sure enough, there was one of Marie's socks. She inspects her case and finds she hadn't zipped one of the pockets. I had taught her to always be polite and she didn't disappoint. She turned to the man and said, "Thanks, I'm glad it wasn't my underwear." As

I said, she didn't disappoint me, she embarrassed me. I told the nice man I wasn't with her.

25. Our return arrival time was changed three times.

We left Wisconsin at 10:00 AM Monday morning, went to Los Angeles and were back in Madison at 7:30 PM Tuesday without a tan or our luggage. I figure the trip cost me approximately $30 per hour. It was an adventure, but never again. I don't care where her boss sends her. This being a caring mother is too much for me. Plus, I can't afford it.

Chapter 19

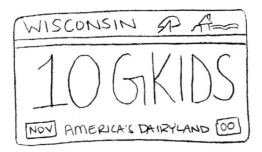

It is difficult to turn off being a mother. At least it must have been for me if I couldn't let my married daughter make a business trip without my supervision. The arrival of grandchildren does help. Once again you have these inquisitive little preteens running around asking you questions and actually listening to your answers.

After we had ten grandchildren and there had been a lengthy stretch without any new ones showing up and with the assurance from our kids that they were "through," we decided to announce to the world that we had ten grandchildren with a license plate "10GKids." But, wouldn't you know, about a year later there was an announcement by our youngest, Marie, that they were expecting a third child.

We didn't go right out and have the license plate changed because "burned once, shame on you, burned twice, shame on me," or something like that. Well, all was forgiven, because we loved the results. Eventually we did change to "11GKids." Since then, we lost a beloved grandson, but have no thoughts of changing back. He is still our beloved grandson and will forever be.

That gang of eleven so far has begat eight great-grandchildren. I'm sure there will be more to come, but we have no intentions of keeping track of them on a license plate.

I love being a grandma and great-grandma. You know that old saying that you like them because you can send them home? There is a lot of truth in that. Parents don't get a down time, grandparents do.

I didn't babysit for my grandchildren on a regular basis while their parents worked. If they really needed me, or if it was a special occasion, I was available. I will never forget one of those babysitting sessions because I'm not that proud of it.

Elizabeth, daughter of our oldest son Chuck, was staying with us for a few days. She was bright, perky, inquisitive, and loved to talk and ask questions – about everything. In fact, when she wasn't sleeping, she was talking. One day she was prattling on while I was trying to concentrate on what I was doing. Apparently her sweet little granddaughter voice had started to grate on me, because suddenly I heard that sweet little voice ask, "Grandma, why does your face look mad?" Talk about feeling like a mean grandma!

Actually, if there had been a choice, I would have skipped kids and gone right to grandkids. The reason being is that our grandkids have always been better behaved than our kids. That was an observation that really bothered me until I read some place that grandkids are more apt to take after their grandparents than their parents. Guilt just lifted away. It was so rewarding to know that all the misdeeds of our four kids were their grandparents' fault. As far as our exceptionally talented, intelligent, beautiful grandchildren, you know who they take after, don't you?

Chapter 20

While sorting through all the stories I have written, I found this one definitely illustrates the difference between my life as a youngster and the lives of our kids and grandkids. The following is an edited version of an article that appeared in a Wisconsin Memories column of the *Wisconsin State Journal* many years ago:

Recently our daughter was telling about taking her two children, ages four and almost six, to see Santa. Both of them were too afraid to go near him.

At the time, I was 63 years old and was thinking back to my Santa years when I was also petrified of the jolly old elf.

Every Christmas Eve, Mother and Dad would load me and my four siblings into the car for the short trip to Gram and Pop's (my mother's parents) for supper and a visit from Santa Claus. Of course, we were excited because we knew we would be several gifts richer by the end of the evening, but I also had my annual scary, tummy-tickling feeling.

Gram and Pop lived in a big old farmhouse. Their sons, our two uncles, still lived at home. Supper was served in the kitchen adjacent to the living room that held the big Christmas tree. The door to the living room was kept closed because, as we all knew, "Santa wouldn't stop at our house if he thought we were watching."

The mainstay of our Christmas Eve meal was oyster stew. I didn't like the oysters, but loved the warm, rich creamy broth with lots of little round oyster crackers floating on top. My dislike for oysters was intensified each year by Pop who made a big show of chasing a live one around in his bowl until he caught it and then asking Gram to toss it back into the kettle until it quit swimming.

Invariably, sometime during the meal, one of my uncles would have to make a trip to the outhouse. While he was gone, we'd hear a rattling or thumping on the roof. While my brother and sisters and I sat there listening and trembling, a frightened uncle would come running back inside with tales of seeing and hearing something outside. Then Pop would speculate whether they should get out the shotgun. As usual, one of us kids would bring reason to chaos by hollering, "Maybe it's Santa."

One year I remember hearing a loud knock on the door just behind Pop's end of the table and looking up to see Pop grabbing at the table trying to land his chair back on the floor. I thought then that it was because he had been startled, but years later figured out he had lost his balance reaching back to knock on the door.

Eventually some brave adult would offer to check out the living room. He or she would sneak over to the door, open it slowly, and peek in. It was always with great excitement a report was made that once again, the red-robed rider-in-the-sky had outsmarted us and delivered gifts. Only after all the commotion and sneaky, old Santa was gone could I relax and enjoy the evening.

I can't remember what age I was when Dad finally told me there wasn't a Santa. I was disappointed, but at least I no longer had to be afraid every Christmas. It was then I realized my uncle didn't really have to make that icy trek to the outhouse every year and there was no one to shoot with the shotgun. I also decided it wasn't us kids, but the adults who enjoyed Santa's visit. In fact, I think Pop was more alive on Christmas than any other time of year. Which makes me wonder about something else; I bet there were no oysters swimming in his bowl either.

Santa wasn't the only thing I was kept in the dark about. "Where do babies come from?" was what I wanted to know. No adult I asked seemed to know, but babies kept coming to our house about every two years. I'm still a little ticked that I spent so much time looking in the wood box because someone had hinted that it was the most likely place they'd show up. The following incident was the first clue that babies are not "found":

When a Friday falls on the 13ᵗʰ, doesn't it knock all the TGIF right out of you? I am not superstitious, but I do know for sure that some pretty strange things happened on Friday the 13ᵗʰ, 1939, when I was nine years old, my two sisters were seven and three, and my brother was five years old.

My family was living on a small farm in Columbia County. My dad was only home on weekends. He was a farmer only by marriage and had finally given up trying to make a living at something he knew nothing about. He found foundry work on the night shift at Gishold Machine Company in Madison, Wisconsin, some fifty miles from our home.

The moment I got out of bed that particular Friday the 13th, I sensed something different. For one thing, my mother was cleaning the house, something she only did when we were expecting company and there had been no mention of that.

Mother gave us children a few small tasks, but for the most part and for our own safety, we stayed out of her way. With the speed she was going, one of us could have been hurt or swept out the door.

On one trip to shake her dust mop, Mother saw a stray cat sitting on our doorstep. It was a coal black cat. I recall her muttering something about Friday the 13th and now a black cat, but it meant nothing to me at the time.

Mother's last task was scrubbing the huge kitchen linoleum on her hands and knees. By then it was noon. She called us to lunch and served us each a bowl of home-made soup that she had set to simmer on the wood-burning range earlier. After lunch she told us to wash up and change into our "other" outfits. She combed our hair and explained that we were going to visit our neighbor who lived about a half mile down the road. "You might be staying there for supper, so I want you to remember your manners," she ordered.

I couldn't believe what was happening. Our "other" outfits were only for church. Mother was in such a hurry to get us ready and on the way that we didn't even get a chance to protest or ask why.

"You kids behave and make yourselves useful and, Dorothy, keep an eye on your brother and sisters," she ordered as she pushed us out the door.

Our walk to the neighbor's house was a quiet, sullen one. We couldn't under-stand why we'd just been forcibly shoved out the door of our home. At the time I'd never heard of abandoned waifs, but I'm sure that's how we looked and felt.

The neighbor lady's welcome seemed a little overzealous when she greeted us at her door. She tried to make us feel at home, but we weren't. Suppertime came and went. There was no mention about when or if we were going back home. We didn't bring pajamas, so I assumed we wouldn't be staying overnight.

It was well past our bedtime, however, when we finally saw headlights of a car coming up the long farm driveway. When we saw it was Dad we were as surprised as we were excited to see him. We didn't usually see Dad until Saturday morning when he arrived home after his late Friday night shift.

On the way home he told us he had a wonderful surprise for us. This whole day had been nothing but surprises as far as I was concerned, however, a "wonderful" surprise would be welcome.

As soon as Dad stopped the car, we jumped out and ran to the kitchen door. It felt so good to be home, wonderful surprise or not. The minute we entered the kitchen, we noticed something was different. There, by the warm kitchen range, sat our big old baby cradle. By the dim light of a kerosene lamp we saw that the cradle held a baby.

Mother was in bed looking pale and tired. On the table beside her bed was some horehound candy. Mother told us it was a treat from Doc Gillette. When I finally got to bed that night, I was too excited to go to sleep. The events of the day kept run-

ning through my mind, and I finally started to put two and two together. The reason Mother had been cleaning the house was Dr. Gillette was coming to visit. I recalled how anxious she was to get us to leave and go to the neighbors and how the neighbor lady wasn't surprised when we arrived. Then, Dad came home early and picked us up and now Mother was in bed looking very tired and there was a new baby in the cradle. Maybe babies weren't found in the wood box after all.

The next morning, in the bright daylight, we really got a good look at our new baby sister. She had long, coal black hair and lots of it. It was as black as the fur on the stray cat that had been on our doorstep the morning she was born. What a contrast to her four siblings who were fair-skinned at birth and, in my case, completely bald. This new baby's skin was ruddy. Her legs and arms had rolls of fat. Her face was so round and plump she couldn't open her eyes. Strangest of all the birth weight of our new baby sister, Mary Louise, on a Friday the 13th, was 9 pounds and 13 ounces.

Chapter 21

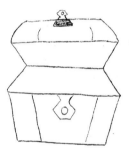

The following story is quite a contrast to the previous one. I titled the piece "Sharon's Box." It won second place in the Wisconsin Writer's Association contest.

It was an unexpected thrill to see Mother's hope chest in a dark corner of the attic. I hadn't thought about that old chest in years. The unfinished pine board box was built by my grandfather and lined in pink floral chintz by my grandmother. As a young girl, Mother had filled it with pretty hand-embroidered linens in hopes of marrying and having a home and family of her own someday. I spied the chest while helping my stepmother clean out the attic of my deceased parents' home.

Mother passed away twenty-three years ago at age fifty-eight. A few years later my father remarried. His new bride, along with all her home furnishings and memorabilia, moved into my father's home.

After Dad passed away, my stepmother remained in the house. One day when I stopped by for a visit, she was saying how she didn't know what she was going to do with all the stuff in the house, especially the things that belong to my dad's family.

I offered to help her go through some of the things. It was a dusty job, but it was also a treasure hunt. I never knew what memory the next box would hold: old 78

RPM records, outdated clothing, papers from school days, photos, old Christmas wrappings, etc. I thought we were finished when I saw the chest. It was too heavy to lift so I decided to simply remove the contents and deal with the chest at a later date.

The chest once held articles of hope and anticipation, but now it held memories of times passed: a couple of ruffled petticoats, yellowed and musty with age, a hand-pieced quilt top, and a photograph of Mother's graduating class from teachers college. At the bottom was a flat, rectangular, white box with a pink bow imprinted in the center. On the bow were the words, "Fleurs Deluxe Cold Cream Soap." I was tired, hot and dirty, so I just lifted the box and a few other items and put them in my car.

When I got home, I carried everything to the basement for later inspection. Everything, that is, except the flat, white box with the pink bow. I sat down for a breather and lifted the cover from the box. I had forgotten. There lay a birth certificate, yellowed with age and fragile to the touch. It read: "Sharon Elizabeth, born in Madison General Hospital on the 23rd day of May A.D., 1945 at 3:00 P.M." It was signed by the attending physician and my father and mother. At the bottom was a gold hospital seal and a print of Sharon's tiny foot. Sharon was my baby sister.

I was thirteen years old in 1945. I recalled how I came home from school and was told by a neighbor that Mother had just been rushed to the hospital by ambulance.

Mother had announced that morning before us kids left for school that she was going to start spring house cleaning and planned to wash the kitchen walls. The ladder was still standing in the middle of the kitchen floor.

It wasn't long before Dad called with the news that we had a new baby sister. "Because she came early, she will have to stay in an incubator until she's bigger and stronger," he explained.

I held the birth certificate for a long time as the memories of that day ran through my mind, finally laying it aside so that I could look at the rest of the contents.

There was a partially used package of birth announcements. I opened a folded piece of newspaper thinking it was a copy of the published birth announcement, but it was a cutout of an infant's romper. Mother must have seen the romper on someone's baby and traced a pattern so she could make one for her expectant child.

In the corner, stuck to the bottom of the box, was a small, discolored bar of castile soap. It's shape distorted by the excessive attic heat. I lifted it to my nose. It had a slightly rancid odor. Next to the soap was a short piece of pink ribbon.

There were several opened envelopes addressed to my parents. They were cards of congratulations. I read several of them until I saw the words "Sincere Sympathy."

Tears came to my eyes as I remembered Mother in her grief and how sad and quiet our house was after Sharon died. "She was born too early!" was the only explanation offered to us kids. Death, like pregnancy, was not discussed with the youngsters in our household.

Sharon never left the hospital. Mother and Dad were the only ones who saw her. There was no church service, just a graveside ceremony, which my siblings and I did not attend. My parents grieved silently and alone.

I laid the rest of the cards aside. Under them was a small book titled "Story of Our Baby." There were blanks to be filled in with information about date of birth, name of hospital etc. One page asked for marks of identification: Hair, light brown.

Eyes, blue. Complexion, dark. Weight, 4 lbs 2 oz. Length, 18 in. There were additional pages, but they were all left blank and I felt as sad and empty as those pages.

Now I have children and grandchildren and can more easily relate to my parents' sadness. I haven't experienced a loss of a child, but after losing a grandson, I knew the agonizing feeling of losing a piece of yourself.

That one small, flat box with a pink ribbon touched me more than anything else I found that day. There were many bits and pieces of family members' lives in that attic, but for Sharon there was just one box, 11 inches long, 9 inches wide and 2 inches deep. The white box with a pink ribbon selected by Mother and filled with all there was and would ever be of her little girl, Sharon.

Chapter 22

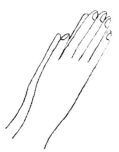

There are funny times and happy times to write about, but as everyone knows, there are also sad times. The following article is about the death of my mother and father:

Standing by the hospital bed of my terminally ill mother, her wasted body about the size of a 10-year-old child, was an experience that will never leave me. My brother, sister and I took turns sitting with Mother nights while Dad was at work. He was at her bedside every day. Each one of us wondered who would be on duty when death came, each hoping down deep we wouldn't be the one, but we kept the vigil so she wouldn't be alone in those final moments.

I can remember wanting to pray, but what should I pray for? The cancer had spread throughout her body causing unbearable pain and destruction. To pray for an end seemed most compassionate, but that meant losing her. I didn't want to lose her. She was only fifty-eight and had so much to live for. There would be more grand-children, great-grandchildren and most importantly there was Dad – what would he do? Her family would be the losers. We all still needed her.

Not being able to find the right words to pray was so uncharacteristic of me. I had always been able to pray spontaneously. When I needed guidance or support any time of day or night, or just felt like thanking Him for a beautiful day, I could pray. Now, when I needed to pray most, I couldn't come up with the right words. I wanted to pray for her to live, but Mother's body was no longer vital. Would she want to live? What I really, really wanted was for none of this to have happened, but it had.

The other emotion I struggled with seems strange to me now. Most of the patients on Mother's floor were terminal. Death was all around us. We saw the same strained faces in the halls and waiting room for several days running, and then one day they would be missing. How presumptuous of me to think my prayers should be answered when so many other loving, praying families had lost their loved one.

I recalled hearing someone say, "Be careful what you pray for because you might get it." What should I pray for?

This dilemma continued to haunt me months after Mother's death. I was back to my usual spontaneous praying and couldn't believe I was so paralyzed when Mother was ill. Suddenly, one day, it came to me. I had been saying the right prayer every day for years. "Thy will be done!" The end of the Lord's Prayer. I'd been saying those words, without thinking about their meaning. I was so elated that I wrote the following poem/prayer:

THY WILL BE DONE, AMEN

A search for guidance,
confused and lost;
I want to pray,
but what do I say?

Failure, rejection
and loneliness;
I want to pray,
but what do I say?

In times of heartbreak,
in times of pain;
I want to pray,
but what do I say?

A loved one dying,
A child in peril;
I want to pray,
but what do I say?

When thought seems to fail,
and words won't come,
all I need say is,
Thy Will Be Done, Amen.

Besides relieving my burden, the poem/prayer has helped others. It was read at a friend's mother's funeral. A seriously ill friend posted it on her refrigerator door. I had it made into bookmarks and sent it out to people when they were hurting. The prayer doesn't say anything new. It is just a reminder. I was trying too hard to find the words. I should have know the Lord doesn't expect eloquence or profundity, He just expects us to ask and trust.

My father lived several years after the passing of my mother. He remarried and had a good life, but he was never as happy as when Mother was alive. He eventually also spent several days in the hospital before his death. Again my siblings and I took turns staying with him. This time I could pray, simply asking that "Thy Will Be Done."

Wisconsin winters can be bitterly cold, but on February 9, 1987, the day my father died, it was unusually warm. After the call came that he had passed away, I tried filling time with mundane tasks. I was washing dishes and looking out the kitchen window above the sink and saw kids running and laughing as they tried to get a kite to fly. They were taking advantage of the beautiful warm winter day. I watched them for a long time and suddenly was struck by the contrast of my sadness and their happiness. How could the rest of the world be feeling so good and having so much fun when I felt so sad?

I sat down, there was music playing on the radio and I started tapping my foot in rhythm while I sat grieving and conjuring the words in the following poem:

My Father is Dying

Two hawks shouldn't be free soaring,
In today's so perfect sky.
The day shouldn't be blue-shining
Enticing me with its warm high.

Benny's music shouldn't be inviting,
Tempting my feet to tap.
Neighbors shouldn't be outside walking
Watching children's kites so high.

There should be no wind tempting hawks to fly.
There should be no sun bright and warming.
There should be no music urging feet to dance.
There should be no kites in the sky.

Why is it only my heart that is grieving?
Why is the music urging my feet to dance?
Why should life go untouched?
Why don't I see some sign?

Yet now, across the darkening sky is streaming
A wash of colors, intense and unique.
Is it nature's salute to him who died?
Is it her answer to the forever why?

Chapter 23

I met so many wonderful, talented people in my writing class. One lady in particular really impressed me. She was tall, probably in her late 70s, with beautiful white hair piled into a bun atop her head. Her name was Clara.

Clara wrote beautiful, moving poetry for class that amazed us because we were aware she had a lot of sadness in her life. We knew that she had moved out of her beloved family home because of family problems and it was obvious she was under some kind of stress.

One day I got the idea that I wanted to write a story about my grandma and the many uses of her apron. Every housewife I knew when I was a kid wore an apron. It was not only a garment to protect their dresses, but was useful in so many other chores. My grandma was no longer living so I would have to find a "grandma." Clara would be the perfect fill-in for the project, but because she always appeared so private, I wasn't sure if I should ask her to be my "grandma" model. After all, she was probably not that much older than me. I finally decided to bite the bullet and ask. I'm so glad I did, because she was absolutely thrilled to help.

When I explained my idea about Grandma's apron and the many chores it was used for, she was completely sold. In fact, she suggested that we have the photo shoot at a museum, because they would have all the antique props.

We set a date and got permission from the museum. I drove to her house and picked her up. Not only was she ready, but she was wearing a blue and white gingham apron she made especially for the occasion. We took photos of tasks performed with an apron. I wrote an article, titled it "My Colorful Memories Of Grandma's Apron" and submitted it to *Reminisce Magazine*. Following is the article:

The only time Grandma was without an apron was when she was in bed or at church. They were of many colors and designs, made from remnants, washed and re-washed flour sacks, or often from what was left of a worn-out dress. They were ample and serviceable and worn as she performed household chores.

The apron helped with tough duties like opening a tight Mason jar and with gentle tasks like wiping a tear from a grandchild's eye. The apron was big enough to keep Grandma's dresses clean and to provide a hiding place for shy toddlers when a stranger came to visit.

Grandma's day started at dawn, when she'd fill her apron with kindling from the woodshed to get a fire going in the kitchen cook stove.

When the men folk came in from morning chores to eat breakfast, the apron protected Grandma's hands while she carried a hot platter to the table.

After breakfast, while Grandma was tidying up the house, the apron became a catchall as she dusted; mislaid safety pins were pinned into a chain hanging from her apron bib. Stray marbles, puzzle pieces, etc. were dropped into the ample pocket.

After the house was in order, it was time to think about dinner. On her way out-doors to pick fresh garden peas, Grandma might notice a spot of dust she'd missed and wipe it away with a corner of her apron.

The screen door was often covered with flies, so as Grandma went out she vigor-ously flapped her apron to shoo away the pesky insects.

In the garden, Grandma's apron was better than a basket for holding peas.

After dinner dishes were done, Grandma sat in her rocking chair, lifted her apron to wipe away the perspiration, then flapped it up and down like a fan to re-fresh herself during the midday heat. Before long, she dropped off to sleep.

After a short nap, it was back to work for Grandma and her apron. The apron was used to move a family of kittens from under a piece of farm machinery the men would be needing in a day or two and to carry away a clutch of eggs that some con-trary hen had laid in the corner of the horses' feed box.

That evening, just as Grandma was about to sit for a spell, a neighbor lady came calling. Grandma quickly untied her apron, lifted it over her head, turned it clean-side-out and put it back on as she went out the door to greet her visitor.

After a nice chat, the neighbor got up to leave and Grandma walked her to her car. It was a cool evening, so Grandma lifted the skirt of her apron, wrapping it around her bare arms to ward off the chill. Of course, this revealed the dirty side of the apron, but it didn't matter...the neighbor knew all the same tricks.

The next morning Grandma would have a fresh, clean apron and be ready for another day.

When I got word from *Reminisce* saying my article had been accepted, I was thrilled. It's always an ego boost to have an article accepted, but this time I was thinking about Clara. I couldn't wait to call her. She had been ill since we worked on the project and I was sure this news would perk her up, and it did. She was so thrilled and wanted to know when it would appear in the magazine, but the publishers hadn't given me a date.

Unbelievably and sadly, Clara passed away before the magazine published *our* article. I was so thankful that she at least knew that it had been accepted.

I called her only child, a son, when I received my copy and he was thrilled, but also regretful that his mother was not alive to enjoy her moment of fame. Clara would have been as pleased as I was when I opened the magazine and saw a quarter-page-sized photo of her with her beautiful white hair in a bun atop her head and wearing the blue checked apron she'd sewn for the occasion. She was holding the corners of the apron skirt together to form a container for some freshly picked garden peas. Asking her to be a model was definitely the right thing to do.

One of the great pluses of having an article published is the notes you receive from people who enjoy reading it. I received several after "Grandma's Apron." The following is an excerpt from one of those notes:

I was very interested in the article in the recent issue of Reminisce *and the story you wrote about your grandmother and her aprons.*

If that isn't a picture of Clara (?), I'll eat my hat!! She and I worked together many years ago and I spent some time with her in her lovely home. Only thing is, her job (at that time) didn't quite fit in with the picture you draw of her always being in the home with the day starting at dawn, etc. So, I am a little mystified - perhaps Clara had a twin sister! But I remember her so well, a lovely, gracious person and the distinctive way she wore her hair. Can you solve this mystery?

I answered her letter and informed her that Clara was a stand-in for my story.

I also got a request from a Baptist church in the State of Oregon asking if they could reprint my "apron" story in their church newsletter. I granted them permission and was happy the article merited reprinting. Clara, if you're listening, "You did good!"

Chapter 24

I love to cook, I can crochet a fancy doily, knit a warm afghan, cultivate a garden, land a fish and rock babies to sleep, but there was a time when I ran up against a real bull, or was it a bear?

I joined an investment club. Never in my life have I felt so inadequate or stupid. I may not have Alzheimer's, but for sure I have half-zheimer's where managing money is concerned. The Beardstown Ladies and their investment club were big news at the time and I figured if they could do it, so could I – not!

At the first meeting, I found to become an intelligent stock investor you must study the stocks and become your own stockbroker. I had to learn to read a Value Line Page and Standard and Poor's graphs, charts and numbers, plus information about a company's past, present and future. From now on, instead of reading novels, I had to read *The Wall Street Journal*, *Money Magazine* and *Barrons*.

It is important to know a company's price earnings ratio, sales growth, sales potential, and ratings within the industry. There are DRP stocks, blue chip stocks, penny stocks and over-the-counter stocks. Should I buy, sell, or hold is a critical concern.

I was overwhelmed. Why did I, a 66-year-old woman, with at least half her brain enjoying involuntary retirement, expect to learn in a two-hour session once a month what stockbrokers and financial planners study for years to learn?

While faithfully reading *The Wall Street Journal*, I found that a regular feature pits three or four financial experts against a dartboard for predictions. The dartboard's stock pick wins a good share of the time. Should I learn something from this?

Compared to other people's problems. this may seem trivial, but I must say I feel much better for having written about my dilemma. I am through with all the grief and self-deprecation and no longer feel overwhelmed or befuddled. In fact, I am thinking more clearly now than I have since my first investment club meeting. I have focus, purpose and goals, and to support my newfound philosophy, I'm going right out to buy myself a dartboard.

Chapter 25

When you like to cook and you write a cookbook, people just naturally assume you know everything there is to know about cooking and related activities. A good example of my supposed knowledge was tested at a niece's wedding.

It was a beautiful day, a beautiful wedding, a beautiful bride. Everything was as it should be – until the reception. The wedding cake was nowhere to be found.

Phone calls were made to the cake baker who worked from her home, but no answer. The guests were seated and served a lovely entrée, but the cake table with the beribboned cake knife and plates was missing a very important item – the cake!

The cake lady finally returned the call, but it was not good news. There had been a mix-up on the date. There was no cake. The bride was crushed.

Suddenly, the bride's older sister came running up to me, demanding, "Aunt Dorth, we've got to do something!"

Think of something? Me? I always bought one of those cards of preformed candy letters and candleholders for my own kids' birthday cakes. She was desperate. She wanted a cake for her sister. There just has to be a photo of the bride and groom cutting their cake and then smashing it into each other's faces.

She dragged me into the kitchen hoping we could find something, anything. All we found were stacks of dirty dishes and a lot of leftover mashed potatoes. Someone sure messed up on that estimate, but that just might be the answer to the cake problem.

I took mashed potatoes and mounded and molded them into three tiers. One of the punch bowls with pink foamy sherbet punch was sitting nearby. Did that look like icing? I thought it did and it was. By now I was getting help. The servers and my niece were getting into the swing of things. We were smearing pink foam on the mashed potato cake. Someone ran out into the dining room and snatched some flowers out of a table centerpiece. Someone else found a ribbon and a couple bows. It wasn't long before we had a "wedding cake."

Someone went into the dining room and told the bride and groom to stand together by the empty cake table. I then made an entrance with a three tiered mound of pink mashed potatoes proudly displayed on a plastic ice cream pail lid. The crowd cheered and the bride's sad face broke into a look of surprise. They had a cake to cut while cameras snapped away. If the photographer didn't focus too closely, maybe the pitiful substitute for a cake wouldn't be noticed. The bride and groom even got a picture of them pushing mashed potatoes in each other's face.

A cake with fresh flowers and icing ribbons could not have gotten a bigger reception. There was happiness on the bride's face the remainder of their evening. She didn't realize it at the time, but she would have a wedding tale to tell unlike any other bride. Not only that, I didn't charge them a cent.

It was so much fun. A big disaster turned into lots of laughs. And, best of all, I picked up two future orders for wedding cakes.

Chapter 26

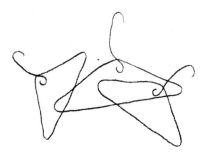

For the most part I've been writing about things I like to do, so I decided to talk about what I don't like to do: shopping! I don't mind grocery shopping, but that's it. When I go to a mall, I go directly to a particular store, straight to the right department, pick out what I want, pay for it, and I'm gone. But when I have to buy a gift for someone else, I have to shop, and that was what I was doing on this particular day.

What in the heck is going on? The place is a zoo. I hate big superstores and today I can tell I'm really going to hate it.

It was early afternoon on a Thursday, not a Thursday before a holiday, just a plain Thursday. There were lines everywhere, carts parked in aisles, store employees restocking. It was bedlam.

One thing I noticed in particular was the unusual number of exuberant young men shopping. They stuck out like a sore thumb. You just don't often see young males shopping and seemingly enjoying it, and at least some of them were. The guys shopping with who appeared to be their parents were not having quite so much fun.

I heard two of the parentless shoppers discussing what to buy as we toured the household soaps and cleanser aisle. One said, "I'm not going to waste money on cleaning stuff."

His buddy replied, "Let's at least get something to clean that cruddy sink; it makes me sick."

That is when it dawned on me. The reason for so many young shoppers was the start of the university school year. They were shopping to stock their home away from home. One young man must have moved into an apartment where the walls, carpet, bathroom fixtures, etc. were all the same color. I couldn't quite get the shade, but it started with an "f" and ended with "ing."

Moms were helping some of the shoppers. They weren't having as much fun. Mom was doing the shopping so instead of chips, popcorn, and candy bars, their carts were filled with cleaning supplies, whole wheat bread, cereal and fresh fruits and veggies.

I heard one mom say, "You wait here while I go look for clothes hangers."

Her six-foot son yelped in complete dismay, "Clothes hangers?"

I had everything I needed and it was time to get out of this madhouse. I headed for the checkout counter. I didn't have to go far. The lines were coming to meet me. They extended down between almost every aisle.

Shoppers were complaining, wondering what was going on. Some couldn't or wouldn't wait and just abandoned their full shopping carts.

When I finally got within eyesight of checkout, it was obvious the surge of customers had taken its toll on the checkers and baggers. They looked beat. I heard the young woman bagger say to the checker, "Are you sure this isn't Saturday?"

The employees weren't alone in looking beat. Magazines at the end of the checkout station were looking pretty dog-eared. Customers were reading magazines while waiting in line and then restocking them.

I'm sure there were some tired store employees that night and lots of partying students. I just hope the guys who bought all the good stuff will invite the poor guy who had to buy the clothes hangers.

And then there was the following shopping trip:

It isn't often I am content to just sit and wait, but if I'm in a bustling public place with lots of people, I find it quite entertaining. In this instance, I was sitting outside a fitting room in a men's clothing store. Charlie was having a suit fitted.

It wasn't long before I noticed a male shopper acting suspiciously. The easiest way to describe him would be to say he looked just like one of the hoods in a mafia movie. He was heavy-set, dark, with slicked-back, greasy hair and a five o'clock shadow. His open trench coat revealed a crumpled suit and tie. Definitely a criminal type.

The thing that caught my eye was the way he was fingering the merchandise instead of looking at it. His eyes were too busy scanning his surroundings. The open trench coat was also suspicious because I read somewhere that loose fitting clothing made it easy for shoplifters to conceal merchandise.

The only clerk available in this particular area was in the dressing room marking Charlie's suit for alterations. I didn't want to leave for fear I would lose track of the obvious shoplifter. He continued walking from display to display, feeling and groping the merchandise while holding them against his stomach. I was sure he must be trying to tuck them inside his coat, but I never actually saw anything disappear.

Finally, Charlie and the clerk returned to the store area. I could hardly wait to tell him about the crook. As I pointed out the culprit and explained his odd behavior, I didn't get the reaction from the clerk that I expected. He just laughed and explained that I had just fingered the store detective. Wouldn't you think a reputable store would have the decency and good sense to hire detectives who don't look like the mafia? I guess I had better stick to people watching and leave the detecting to someone else.

Chapter 27

No place and nobody is off limits when I have to come up with something for writing class, not even the hallowed halls of our church and its members are safe:

Easter is a day of joy for churchgoers. For me, I hope it will provide my weekly offering for creative writing class. As is the custom, Charlie and I arrived at church early because of the annual standing-room-only Easter visitors. That gives me plenty of time to people watch.

A little girl came skipping down the aisle, her fancy Easter bonnet bouncing on top of her head. When she saw Grandma sitting in a pew where she was saving seats for her family, she took off running and gave Grandma a big hug.

The female half of a couple sitting in front of us was distracted before and during the service with her male partner's shoulder length, wavy hair. She was constantly rearranging it with her fingers. Apparently it wasn't working, because she nudged him and using herself as a model, she gave him instructions on how to repair his hairdo. I thought it looked okay, but then there's a bald guy sitting next to me.

In front of the hair-impaired man was a little girl, about four years old, who had more energy than one little body could hold. She wiggled, squirmed, whined and talked out loud. Once when she was talking to Mom, it was obvious Mom was more interested in her daughter's bangs than what she was saying. She must have spotted a straggler because she reached to her daughter's forehead and with one mighty yank, pulled it out. The surprised kid grabbed her head and let out a yelp. No wonder she moved around a lot. She didn't dare sit still by her mother or she'd be bald.

During our service, we have a segment during which a Sunday school teacher holds court with the children up by the altar. The Easter-themed question she asked the children was whether they ever had something so wonderful happen to them that they couldn't wait to tell everyone about it. One little girl said she wished for a doll in her Easter basket this morning and she got her wish. Of course that was the start of a trend and we listened while five or so children told about the candy, Beanie Babies, etc. they found in their baskets. One little guy was really ticked off as he wanted a Star Wars character and he got a "chicken walker" instead. No one around seemed to know what a chicken walker was, but it sounded like a poor substitute.

The teacher tried to turn the conversation around to something more meaningful and to the theme of the day by asking if, other than Easter baskets, was there something wonderful that happened in the past week. One boy announced that his mom was going to have a baby. Another said that his cousin, who had been in the hospital for a long time, was finally home. The teacher noted how wonderful all that was and then went into the story of Easter. They appeared completely engrossed in what she was saying until one little boy raised his hand and, when called upon, announced that he could "burp a lot." The teacher promised him she would discuss it with him later.

Once the minister stood to give the sermon, I was sure the funny stuff was over, but he said he had a story to tell also. He told about a sweet lady, a member of a nearby church, who had died recently. She was 90 years old and had never married or, as the minister put it, "this little old spinster had never known the joys of marriage."

Thinking that was the punch line, I started laughing, but I was the only one who got the joke and the minister was still talking. I got control of myself and listened as he continued. The lady had left detailed instructions to the church about how she wanted her funeral to be conducted. The strangest request was that there be no male pallbearers. Her reasoning, she explained, was, "They didn't take me out when I was alive and I'll be darned if I'll let them do it when I'm dead."

Hooray, the minister just gave me a perfect ending to my written assignment this week. A blessed Easter to all.

Chapter 28

Why do most regular churchgoers sit in the same pew every week? Some don't, but most do and Charlie and I are one of the "dos." We don't sit there because we want to be with our best friends. In many cases, the only time we see our church seatmates is in church. Such is the case of my seatmate who was the subject of the following story I titled "Spring Birdies":

There are few residents of the United States mainland who are more appreciative of signs of spring than Midwesterners. Signs certainly don't guarantee warm weather, but they give us hope. The return of birds from the South are one of our first and most noticeable predictors of warm weather. We thrill at the sight of the first robin, red-winged blackbird, etc. Seeing the goldfinch slowly turn from olive-drab to a yellow as bright as the summer sun is a colorful promise of warmer days. Then, of course, there is the annual appearance of that prolific spring bird, the Links Cuckoo.

The Links Cuckoo is difficult to identify because, like a mockingbird that sings many songs, the Links Cuckoo wears many colors. Their unusual call, a loud, panicked "fore, fore," is one clue to their identity. However, a more positive characteristic is the stick they hold and the strange heads-down position in which they stand while looking at a small round object at their feet. No, the stick isn't for a nest and the object is not an egg. It is a small, round dimpled thing called a golfball.

In early April, I attend a luncheon at the golf club near our house. As we were leaving, I noticed the cement walkway was wet, but I could see golfers on the course so I assumed the rain had passed. I was wrong; they were golfing in the rain. Golfers might be a sign of spring, but not a sign for weather.

In church one Sunday, I was talking to the man sitting by me. I knew he had retired and that he and his wife lived on a lake, so when I asked him how he was spending his retirement, I expected to hear about the fish he'd caught or time spent boating. "It's great!" was all I got.

"Do you do any fishing?" I asked in spite of his apparent disinterest.

"No! We used to sail, but we don't do that any more."

Then, as if to explain his lack of water activities, he said, "I've taken up golf."

He then went on to tell me how frustrating the game was. So that was what was wrong with him. This man worked for years as a rough, tough, self-assured police detective who always appeared cool and in control.

"You know," he said as if reading my mind, "I always considered myself a cool-headed person. I never let my nerves get to me, even when called out on some pretty risky crime scenes. I could calmly and systematically go through a mental checklist and by the time I arrived on the scene, I was ready for anything. Now all I have to do is grip the handle of a stupid golf club and I break out in a cold sweat. Just looking down at that miserable little white ball can make my hands shake and my knees go limp."

In fact, he went on, he had been golfing on Saturday and came home so upset he didn't know whether he would go to church on Sunday. He was beginning to blame his Maker for his problems.

He was on a roll, "One day I dubbed an easy approach shot that sent me into a childish tirade. When I turned, I saw two middle-aged ladies who were probably close enough to me to have witnessed my tantrum. It was a moment of shame. When they got closer, I apologized for my language and actions and started to explanation how frustrated I was, but they came off short with a sympathetic, 'We understand!'"

When this church friend started golfing, the only smile his wife saw for days at a time were the ones on his golf balls. He butchered so many of them he wasn't sure he could afford to play. Then he heard that the company would replace each damaged ball if he mailed them in. He sent them his first batch and got replacements with a note apologizing for the problem. With the second shipment came a note suggesting that perhaps the problem was something other than a ball deficiency. Their diagnosis wasn't lost on my above-average-intelligence duffer friend, who in turn suggested to them it might be more cost effective for them if they sent him an instructor.

I really do believe golf is a health hazard. It can turn a happy adult into a brooding, blubbering wimp. My church buddy is proof of that. What a gold mine a golf course would be for psychiatrists. There are probably enough patients on the course on any given day for a golfing shrink to write off a whole summer of golf. Maybe along with a course pro, golf courses and clubs should have an in-house psychiatrist.

To conclude this essay on Links Cuckoos, I have decided they are not the brightest birds around. New ones tee up every year and the old ones just keep putt, putt, puttin' along. So, next year, when the last snow falls, or maybe even before, start listening for that plaintive call, "fore, fore," a signal that once again the spring birdies have returned.

Chapter 29

For many years, the first trip of the year to the cottage was to make maple syrup. Charlie's Uncle Sam who lives in Wisconsin's North Woods would alert us when the sap started to run and we'd be on our way. The following article, and renditions thereof, have appeared in four different magazines and newspapers and won an award in a state writing contest:

The call we'd been waiting for finally came. Charlie's Uncle Sam phoned to say he had tapped a few maples and the sap was running. The forecast for the next few days was daytime temperatures in the high forties to low fifties, and night temps in the low thirties – perfect syrup weather.

The maple trees had nothing on us once we got the call. We could feel our own juices moving around also. All but perishables had been packed in waiting. The syrup season is not a set time, so when the sap runs, we run.

After a five-hour drive, we pulled onto the dirt road leading to the cottage and knew we were in for a tough time. The snow on the road had melted, leaving it muddy and full of ruts, but in the woods there was still a couple feet of wet snow. Going from tree to tree collecting sap was going to be a struggle.

After we opened the cottage and unloaded the car, the next order of business was tapping trees. Charlie drilled the holes with a hand drill, placed a sterilization tablet in each hole and then tapped in a spigot. I followed along and hung buckets.

The first containers I hung were three-pound tin coffee cans we'd strung with a wire handle. Part of the thrill of making syrup is listening to the music of the multi-pitched plink-plunks of the first drips of sap in the empty metal buckets.

When I ran out of coffee cans, I hung plastic buckets along with commercial sap sacks. The sacks are more practical because they hold more sap and the sealed bags keep out bugs, twigs etc. However, the buckets are free and reusable.

After tapping the trees, we were wet and weary from trudging through the heavy, thawing snow. There was ice water in our boots and our hands were freezing. It was time to go inside, eat and go to bed. Tomorrow would be a busy day.

It's exciting checking the buckets in the morning. Sometimes they are spilling over and sap sacks are bulging. Often there is a skimming of ice topping the sap and icicles hanging from over-full buckets. Other mornings we find little or nothing has dripped during the night. It all depends on the temperature. If it doesn't drop, sap won't drip.

After breakfast, we hauled the cooking pan up from the basement and washed it. A path has to be shoveled through the snow from the woodpile to the firebox.

We are proud of the firebox that Charlie made out of a discarded fuel oil tank. He laid the oval-shaped monstrosity on its side and cut off what then became the top and reinforced it. We lined it with firebrick, put a chimney pipe at one end and sliding doors for feeding the fire at the other end. Charlie's sheet metal fabrication shop built a stainless steel cooking pan that exactly fit the opening cut in the side of the tank.

Next we set a roaring fire in the firebox so it would have a good start once we were ready to begin cooking down the day's collection of sap.

After the cooker is ready, we each take two five-gallon buckets and make the rounds from tree to tree. The snow, which is usually thawing during the day, crusts over at night and collecting is a real athletic feat. In some places the crusted snow supports us, but without warning, we'll hit an air pocket and sink into the snow up over our boots. There we stand, buckets of sap in each hand, snared in an icy trap. It takes a mighty tricky juggling act to keep our balance while trying to free our legs.

When we get enough sap to start cooking, we place the pan on the firebox over the roaring fire. Then, quickly, before the pan gets too hot, pour in the sap. Next it's wait, watch, feed the fire and skim foam off the top of boiling syrup.

The object is to boil the sap down as fast as possible to insure a honey-colored grade-A syrup. The dark colored maple syrup sold in stores would never win a prize in a syrup competition. Not that we haven't produced some dark syrup occasionally. I'm sure it happens to anyone who cooks syrup over an open fire without benefit of automatic temperature control. We have been lucky however, to have never burned syrup beyond use. The dark syrup is used in baked beans, cookies, breads, or candy.

While we wait for the sap to boil down, we enjoy the spring show. Birds and animals are beginning to do their spring thing. In their excitement and dedication to duty, they aren't the least bit concerned about our presence. We get a kick out of chickadees landing on our hats to steal the seed we put there for them.

Some years we've seen bald eagles fly over, loudly announcing the start of a new season at their summer home. A real show-stopper is seeing and hearing an osprey on the wing break a branch out of the top of one tree and add it to the unkempt mish-mash of branches for this year's new nest in the top of another tree.

The cooker becomes the hub of existence for syrup makers. We gather around it for warmth and to dry wet clothing. The steam that rolls up off the boiling sap entices us with its delicious maple-y aroma. It's a place to rest, converse or daydream. We get full measure of energy from the fire, roasting wieners and marshmallow over it for lunch. A bottle of soda or beer pushed down into a snow bank keeps our drinks cool and hot maple syrup drizzled over clean, white snow makes a delicious snow cone.

If the snow is deep enough, we cut out icy benches where we can sit by the fire and rest our weary bones. That's usually a job for a young, healthy, ambitious grandson.

Once the sap begins to show a little color and has boiled down to a shallower depth, we allow the fire to die down. The closer sap gets to syrup, the more the sugar content, the easier it burns. When the sap has reduced down to where it might burn in the large cooking pan, we draw if off through a filter and carry it inside to finish off in smaller pots on the kitchen range where we have more control. After the hydrometer measures just the right density, cooking is finished and it's time for a last filtering through a wool flannel filter, then bottle it and seal it.

When I put the syrup through the final filter, it hurts to see how much of the thick syrup is trapped in the filter. I recall reading how early syrup makers, as part of the salary for their hired help, would give them the syrup-soaked filters at the end of the work day. They would take them home, rinse them into a cooking pot and re-boil the liquid down into syrup.

Making syrup is a great family project and it can be enjoyed by both young and old. We've had three generations of our family joining in, but, because of the work and our ages, we have given up on it. It takes from thirty to forty gallons of sap to make one gallon of syrup, which might give you some idea of just how much work it is. That also explains why 100% pure maple syrup is so expensive.

Every year one of us would hold a bottle of finished syrup up to the light of a window to check the clarity. It was always proclaimed the prettiest syrup we ever made. But the proof is in the tasting and that we did when we poured it over a steaming stack of homemade buttermilk pancakes. It was a taste delight beyond description.

Just because we thought our syrup was extraordinary didn't make it so, but in May of 1991, we had proof. Our entry in the Wisconsin Maple Syrup Festival contest in Aniwa, Wisconsin won a blue ribbon.

This article probably got as much response from readers as any other article I've written. One man wanted exact dimensions for building the firebox. Others just said it brought back so many wonderful memories. For our family, it recorded memories.

Chapter 30

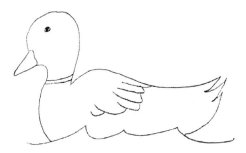

Syrup time might be pretty close to official spring, but when you're walking though a couple feet of snow and the river is still covered with ice, it doesn't feel very springy. The following is what we consider spring in the North Woods:

"I suppose she's telling him she has a headache," Charlie observed.

"She just wants him to check the house for leaks before she makes any commitments," I countered.

We were at the cottage, eating breakfast and watching a pair of wood ducks do their spring thing on the Flambeau River. It was meant to be a work trip, but the fringe benefits in the woods overlooking the river this time of year are so enticing.

Woodland flowers are beginning to stir in preparation for their grand opening. If you stand perfectly still on a quiet, dry day, you can hear the gentle rustling of last fall's crispy maple leaves as the tiny plants beneath them stretch and probe upwards trying to catch a touch of warm sun.

The pretty little blue and white Hepaticas have already poked their heads from under cover, not waiting, as most flowers do, for their leaves to appear first.

We saw a couple of deer grazing on spring's fresh greenery. They were as surprised to see us as we were to see them. They raised their heads when they heard us and watched with cautious curiosity. Suddenly, in unison, as if cued, they flicked their tails and bounded off.

One afternoon we cut up downed trees for next winter's wood supply. Lying on the ground was a sap sack we had missed when pulling taps at the end of this year's syrup season. Inspection of the sack revealed it must have been bulging full when someone with a sweet tooth, most likely Herr Bear, chewed it open to drink the sweet liquid.

Spring brings the return of all sorts of woodland birds. Their calls were all around us announcing that a home had been found and it was time to start a family.

The friendly little Phoebe is busy building a nest under the eaves outside the kitchen window. The family makes a horrible mess on the side of the cottage every year, but watching them is worth the mess.

This spring we have a family of woodchucks in the crawl space beneath the kitchen. A discovery we made the first night after we went to bed and listened to the babies playing tag. They squealed, squeaked, and bumped into the heat ducts with such force that it sounded like they were in, not under, the kitchen.

The next day, we set a live trap baited with vegetables at the entrance to their hole. I looked out the window just above the trap several times that day, but no luck. Was it possible they didn't like our treats? I decided to throw in a couple of cookies, but before I got around to taking them dessert, I took one more peak out the window. There, stretched out on top of the trap, were two young woodchucks sunning themselves. How they got out of that hole without going into the live-trap itself, I don't know. They won; we'd just have to wait until they decided to move out on their own.

Of all the spring things going on, the greatest show of all is the return of the ducks. There are hooded and common mergansers, mallards and, the prize of them all, wood ducks. Mother Nature held nothing back in selecting the colors and design for the magnificent wood duck. Seeing them back on the river this spring is what instigated our comments at the breakfast table that morning.

They were checking out our wood duck box, looking for a spot to raise a family. The male duck had romance on his mind while the female played hard to get.

Mr. Duck swam in circles around Mrs. Duck, dipping his head into the water faster and faster, working himself into a frenzy, then he would rise up out of the water and flap his wings. Mrs. Duck gazed unimpressed, off into space, probably wondering if the nesting box was befitting a duck of her breeding.

Finally, seemingly bored with it all, the female lifted up and flew up river. The male followed. It wasn't long before she came back alone. She sat quietly treading water for a time, maybe just a bit disappointed that her suitor hadn't followed. Again, she flew up river. I don't know where she found him or what she did to rekindle his attention, but this time he returned with her. "It looks like we are going to have tenants again this year," I remarked to Charlie. Our wood duck box had passed inspection.

We worked hard to get all our spring chores done, but what a show while we were doing it. What a privilege to witness the forest, river and seasonal residents once again doing their spring thing. On our next trip, the Hepatica will be gone, but there will be other flowers in their place: trilliums, jack-in-the-pulpit in the woods, marsh marigolds along the nearby stream, etc.

The woodchucks will have moved to their summer home. Mrs. Phoebe will be sitting on eggs or maybe feeding babies. The duck will be settled in the nesting boxes. The deer will have traded their winter grey for a pretty golden tan imitating the sunspots on the trees. Life in the forest always changing yet always the same as it follows Mother Nature's plan.

Chapter 31

In our early cottage years, there were still open pit dumps where local residents disposed of their trash and garbage. It was a system that had its merits. Everyone hauled their trash to the dump and, while they were there, rummaged through their neighbor's junk for things they could use. Charlie's Uncle Sam would look for discarded woolen coats, jackets, trousers, etc. He'd take them home and wash them in an old washing machine he had in his basement just for that particular chore. When they were clean and dry, his wife, Aunt Esther, would cut them into strips and braid them into beautiful area rugs. It was a wonderful system of recycling.

It was a good way to pick up a little gossip too – what medications your neighbors were taking, who was drinking what and how much. There were a lot of liquor bottles and blue Milk of Magnesia bottles in the dump – a cause and effect situation. A good story could be conjured up by going through other people's trash. As for the garbage, black bears cleaned that up at dusk. It was a favorite source of free entertainment for all – Mom, Dad and the kids from the safety of our car.

Even though watching the bears at the dump was exciting, it also made everyone a little nervous because that meant there were *bears* in the area!

Occasionally we'd hear about one breaking into a vacant cottage and trashing it looking for food. We had rules to keep our place bear proof – no garbage or open food left setting out. Dry foodstuff was stored in metal cans and inside closed cupboards. My advice about bears was, "If you see a bear, just holler and clap your hands because they are as afraid of you as you are of them."

It wasn't until many years later, after our children and grandchildren were grown and not eaten by bears, that I found I hadn't given out very accurate information. One morning when I went into the kitchen to make breakfast, I saw a black bear standing on its hind legs having his breakfast at a birdfeeder some ten feet from the window. I opened the window and yelled and clapped my hands. Herr bear turned his head toward me, gave me a sleepy "so-who-are-you" stare and went right on eating. So I lied!

Over the years, we've had a couple of interesting experiences with hibernating bears. One of them happened when we were at the cottage making maple syrup. I wrote the following article about the experience and titled it "What's In A Hole?":

"Why do you two have to know what's down in that hole?" I asked in disgust.

I was talking to Charlie and our son, Steve, who had just made their second trip back to the cottage to get something to help them uncover the mystery of the hole. This time they got a camera and flash. Apparently a flashlight and mirror tied to a string had failed.

This whole escapade actually began the previous fall when Steve and a friend were in the woods bowhunting. They startled a black bear in the process of digging a hole most likely for winter quarters. As soon as the bear saw the two men, it took off.

Now, early the following spring, Steve was wondering whether the bear had returned and finished digging. When he said he was going to check, his dad hollered, "Wait, I'll go with you!"

They found the hole, but the entrance to it looked much too small for a bear. Steve got down on the ground to look inside, but found the hole angled off to one side and all he could see was dirt and roots. They hoped a flashlight and mirror would aid in seeing around the bend. When that didn't work they came back for the camera.

"How do you know if there is even anything down there?" I asked

"We can hear its heartbeat," Charlie answered matter-of-factly.

"If, just by chance, it is a bear, do you think you two should be messing around with it?"

"No way can it be a bear. The hole is too small," was the educated answer as they left with the camera.

Steve's wife, Karen, and our two-and-a-half-year-old granddaughter, Angie, were also at the cottage. Karen and I waited just so long before curiosity got the best of us. We finally had to see for ourselves what they were up to and whether the mystery animal had devoured them.

When we got to the site, Charlie was laying flat on his stomach, his hand and camera down inside the hole. I couldn't believe my eyes. I decided our granddaughter should not be witness to her grandpa's arm being chewed off, so we left.

As we started back to the road, I muttered, "Those two are crazy." Evidently I didn't mutter softly enough, because Angie said, "Two crazy."

Oh well, she'd find out sooner or later.

Before we got back to the road, Charlie and Steve came running up behind us, laughing nervously and panting.

"What happened?" I asked.

"The heartbeat was getting louder."

Apparently, Charlie had aimed the camera in the direction that the hole angled and snapped the shutter three times. After the second snap, the sound he imagined was a heartbeat grew faster and louder. Charlie wasn't sure whether it was his imagination or not, but he thought he might have heard a growling noise.

He snapped one more quick shot. That did it. They didn't have to wonder whether they heard a growling noise or not, this time there was no doubt. That is when they decided to leave. No one can accuse those two of being slow learners.

When Charlie was telling his Uncle Sam about their experience, Sam told them it wasn't a heartbeat they heard, it was an animal, probably a bear, thumping a warning with its feet.

"How about the size of the hole?" Steve asked. "It was too small for a bear."

Sam explained, "The rim of the hole was probably depressed by the heavy winter snow, making it smaller."

We were anxious to get the slides developed to see if they would reveal the answer to the mystery.

When we finally viewed the slides, the first two were shots of dirt walls and roots. The third slide showed two shiny eyes, a shiny muzzle and the big teeth of a black bear. There was some nervous snickering coming from the two adventurers as Charlie commented, "Maybe we shouldn't have been messing around there."

Pretty sharp guys, wouldn't you say?

Chapter 32

T he following story has the same characters as the previous one: Steve, Charlie, and a black bear:

On this occasion, Steve was rabbit hunting when he heard a noise that sounded like a squealing pig. There aren't or shouldn't be pigs in the Flambeau forest, so he was curious about the source and decided to investigate.

A downdraft windstorm that blew through the area a year before had toppled a lot of trees, so walking was difficult. His only compass was an occasional squeal that got louder and louder as he walked.

When he finally got to the source, he couldn't believe his eyes. One of the downed trees had toppled with roots intact, pulling up a huge clump of soil and leaving a large depression in the ground. In that hole, with the root ball of the tree as partial shelter, was a huge, sleepy-eyed mama bear and, by her side, a squealing bear cub. All you could see was a black ball lying next to Mom and an occasional flash of pink as it opened its mouth to squeal. Steve thought there might possibly be two cubs, but didn't want to get close enough to take inventory.

He didn't hang around long. A mama bear is ferociously protective of her young. Her eyes were open, but looked dazed. When I saw her I likened her gaze to the stare of someone who had hit the bottle a bit too heavy the night before.

She was definitely in hibernation this time of year, but how long does it take a sleepy mom bear to wake up if she feels her cubs are in danger? Steve hurried back to the cottage to tell his dad and me. For Charlie it was another "photo op." Out came his camera and away they went. I'm thinking, Not again.

Charlie made several trips to take photos. I accompanied him a few times, but stood back farther than Charlie did while he snapped photo after photo. It was quite a sight. Mama was lying at the base of an uprooted tree and not completely sheltered, so her heavy black coat was covered with snow.

Bear cubs only weigh about eight ounces and they are hairless when they are born. Mama bear keeps them tucked under her and breathes warm air on them to keep their bare little bodies warm and near their food source. The cub(s) we were watching was a little roly-poly ball of black fur by the time we found it.

Mom never moved when we visited, but I decided that she was a lazy mama bear who took the first hole in the ground she found and said, "Night, night." I also decided after the fact that we were lucky that lazy mom didn't decide that we were a little too close for comfort and wake up with a vengeance. Our up close and personal experiences with hibernating bears is not something I would recommend, but they certainly were interesting, once-in-a-lifetime experiences. And again, the photographer got his shot.

Chapter 33

For nearly forty years, I was boss, in charge of the daily routine in our home. Now I face a big change. Charlie is retiring and the big question is: Now who's in charge?

When someone asks him, "What are you going to do with yourself once you retire?" he answers, "Reorganize the kitchen!"

I think that's a joke. I hope that's a joke. Because, if it isn't a joke, it's no joke.

He also says he has some great ideas for "time management." Certainly something to which I will be receptive.

Just how this is going to work out, I'm not sure. I have checked with friends to see if they would take him for a couple of weeks at a time. I had one taker until her husband found out about it. Our kids have already made it perfectly clear he can't move in with them.

We are just going to have to work it out somehow. Each of us will have to be open-minded and tolerant, especially Charlie. He will have to realize that, even though he stakes out straight garden rows for me, they will still end up crooked. If I'm busy writing, he can't ask me, "What's for dinner?" or "Where are my socks?" and other equally urgent questions.

I will have to get used to him setting a dirty dish on the counter directly above the dishwasher instead of lowering it a few inches, opening a door and putting the dish inside. Also, no matter where he goes, or what he does, he will end up with mud on his shoes and track it throughout the house. He is the only man who comes home from church with mud on his shoes.

We both have our own idea about when to run errands. I like to get the housework done first and he would rather do the errand running first.

Somehow I am going to have to come up with a way to predict when he will lose something or want me to assist him with a project before I either answer or make a phone call. This may be one of the tougher problems.

Also, I have to be more in tune to whether a pipe wrench on the dining room table is there because he got it out to use or if that's where it was put after its use. He gets a little testy if he lays a tool down mid-job and I come along and put it away.

Another task before me is to put things where he can find them. Actually, maybe I *should* let him reorganize my kitchen. That way he wouldn't have to open every cupboard door or drawer looking for a fork or drinking glass.

I really do think we will survive this monumental event in our lives. Surely he will find enough to do to keep him from getting bored. In fact, I have, in my own gracious, generous, caring way, drawn up a list of projects just to ward off such a possibility.

As far as who's the boss, maybe we can be co-bosses, or take turns. If I find out what works, I'll write a how-to-book about it.

Chapter 34

HOME OF THE GRIZZLY

V isiting Alaska had been a dream of Charlie's and mine for years. We even set a date at one point, but with four kids who had a habit of wearing clothes and eating, it didn't happen. Years later, when Charlie was going to retire, we decided now was the time. Three weeks after his retirement, we packed the car and were off to Alaska. I wrote "Guests of the Grizzly," an account of one leg of our trip:

Here we are at Brook's Lodge in Alaska's Katmai National Park, going through "bear orientation" to avoid becoming a grizzly meal.

"This is the home of the grizzly and you are guests" was the young warden's opening statement.

"Rule number one, you must stay fifty yards away from one grizzly and one-hundred yards from two," she went on.

"Running can elicit a chase response from otherwise non-aggressive bears. If the bear is aware of you but has not acted aggressively, back away slowly, talking in a calm firm voice while slowly waving your arms. Bears standing on their hind legs are just trying to identify you and are not threatening," she added.

I couldn't quite picture myself face to face with a bear and cooing softly, "Nice bear, nice bear." This was not what a National Geographic TV special had led me to envision.

Our guest cabin was surrounded by tall grasses and shrubs. Flattened grassy areas were evidence that King Grizzly bedded down wherever they wanted. As if to emphasize who was master of this domain, there were claw and teeth marks on the side of our cabin.

Grizzlies are active day and night, so we were told to be constantly alert, as they consider it a threat if startled. To avoid surprise, it was suggested that we clap our hands or sing when hiking. Much to Charlie's chagrin, singing was my bear-scaring method of choice. I tried "The Bear Went Over The Mountain," but was afraid that might attract them. I felt the same about the well-known country song "Oh (Bear)y Me Not On The Lone Prairie," so I finally settled on "Bill Grogan's Goat."

As we walked the grounds, I constantly wondered if I'd remember all the rules in the event I came face to face with a bear. There were no bears taking the orientation classes. Would they know what they were supposed to do in the event of an encounter? Occasionally bears make bluff charges, coming as close as ten feet before stopping and veering off. The instructions in such an event were to stand still until the bear stops and has moved away and then slowly back off. If a grizzly makes contact, we were to curl up in a ball, protecting our stomach and kneel and play dead. However (I hate howevers), if the attack is prolonged, change tactics and fight back vigorously. I wondered how intimidating it would be to a thousand-pound bear if I suddenly uncoiled from a fetal position and applied a karate chop to its nose.

Charlie looked forward to going angling for salmon while at the lodge. The huge fish were an awesome sight, having just turned a brilliant red after spawning as they lay in large schools at the bottom of the crystal clear river. It was a fishing paradise for bear or human, but there were rules for fishing, also.

If you hooked a salmon with a bear nearby, you were to cut your line. The rangers didn't want a repeat of what happened a month earlier. The grizzlies had figured out that the whine of a line running off a fisherman's reel meant dinner was on the other end. A bear would be on the fish in a flash. Because of this, fishing was closed for ten days to give the bears time to forget.

There was a multilevel viewing stand on the banks of the Brooks River for guests to view bears as they swam, fished and cavorted in the water. Just their backs and the tops of their heads were visible as they snorkeled for fish. We were close enough to hear salmon bones cracking and flesh ripping as they ate their catch. People with cameras filled the viewing stand from sunrise to sunset. They came from all over the world, some with unbelievably sophisticated photo equipment and others with their little Instamatics.

After a couple of days without bear confrontations, we became complacent and relied on rangers constantly patrolling the grounds with their two-way radios to keep track of the bears. Besides, by this time, Charlie had forbid me to sing.

One evening at dusk, while walking from the main lodge to our cabin, we saw light flashes coming from around a bend just ahead. As we continued along the path, excited voices and clapping hands accompanied the flashes. It meant only one thing: bears.

When the people came into view, they were facing our way, which meant the bear must be somewhere in between, a realization that too quickly became fact. Plodding clumsily toward us, about twenty-five feet away, was a huge bear, its girth overtaking the width of the path. Aware that we were already breaking rule number one, "stay fifty yards away from one bear," I decided I might as well break rule number two, "don't run," and made a dash for the women's bathhouse a few feet from where I stood.

I've heard you don't know until you're faced with danger whether you're a hero or a coward. I now know. I also found out how easy it was for me to abandon my beloved husband who, after being rejected as a grizzly bedtime snack, asked, "What if the bear had been female and was on her way to the shower?"

In that eventuality, I guess this would be Charlie's story, not mine. The author matters not, the memories of the few days spent as a "Guests of the Grizzly" will long be remembered. Those few days with the bears made our dream trip to Alaska just that – a dream trip.

Chapter 35

After Charlie retired, we bought a home in Port Charlotte, Florida, where we spend about four to five months every winter. Now we can fish all year long. We fish in Charlotte Harbor. We both love it, but one day what we got was not what we were fishing for. I wrote the following article and it appeared in the *Charlotte Sun's WaterLine Magazine*:

This Fishing Trip Was a "Bee"-stly Experience

So you thought we were just out having fun when we didn't stay home and weed the flower gardens? Well, let me tell you, this fishing trip was not fun.

The captain (my husband, Charlie) and I had just baited up and cast our lines in the water when I heard slapping and some nasty words coming from the front of the boat. I looked around to see him swatting at his head trying to ward off a bug looking for a place to land. It wasn't long before the darned thing was buzzing around my head. After a few slaps from me, it turned and went back to Charlie. Then both of us were swatting at the same time as several of the pesky buggers had come aboard. They looked like bees, which meant they could sting us.

"We gotta get out of here," I hollered and, for a change, Charlie agreed with me. We pulled in our lines and he started the motor. I tugged at the anchor and found it was lodged in reef debris. Charlie expertly maneuvered the boat in a circle to dislodge the anchor while we both continued to ward off our attackers.

Finally under way, I moved back to try to wave off the bees that were flying around Charlie's head. When I got to him, I couldn't believe my eyes. The top of his hat was covered with about a four-inch diameter pile of squirming, buzzing bees.

Now, I'm not brave, but neither can I captain a boat, so I had to save Charlie. For lack of not knowing what else to do, I gingerly lifted his hat, bees and all, off his head and tossed it into the harbor, I felt I had just committed an extremely courageous act, but little credit did I get: "That's my fishing hat, grab the net!"

Apparently that hat was more important than trying to avoid getting stung, but true to my unselfish nature, I grabbed the net and snagged his precious bonnet – still covered with live bees.

Now what? I remembered that we had a bucket stashed in one of the compartments for some purpose or another. I took a roll of toilet tissue out of it (does that give you a clue?) and carefully dropped the hat, bees and all, inside and sealed it up. Surely sitting in an airtight container in the hot sun for about an hour while we returned home would result in a bucket of steamed and dead bees.

As soon as we were at the dock, Charlie opened the bucket to check his hat and the hardy little buggers were still running around healthy as could "bee." We were lucky, as the only real damage resulting from our harrowing experience was a wet hat doused in bug spray and a bent anchor. Catch of the day: bees!

Chapter 36

Part of growing old is health problems. Bodies just wear out. Charlie recently had a serious health problem. He started losing strength in his right leg and was running a high fever. The diagnosis was that he had contracted a serious infection during an earlier surgical procedure. As a result, he was scheduled for an infusion every day for two months, which meant we would not be leaving home for more than a few hours at a time. Charlie had to use a walker to get around so it was easier to sit. Life was boring.

One thing we really missed was going to our cottage, but there was no way Charlie could get around up there using a walker. The whole plot is situated on a slope, so we are always either going down hill or climbing up hill in uneven terrain.

When Charlie finally had his last infusion, we decided to take a chance and head north. We felt if Charlie got down the hill to the cottage, he could just stay there. Sitting on the porch watching and listening to the river and the wind in the trees would be a welcome change.

It rained the last half of the trip and was still raining when we arrived. That made sitting on the porch even more fun. We listened to the rain in the trees and were so happy to be anywhere but sitting in our house at home.

That night when we went to bed, we were a little worried. The river was rising. If it rained all night, we might lose our pier. There was nothing we could do about it, so we went to bed and hoped.

The next morning our biggest fears had come true. The water had reached the wood sections on top of the metal pier frame. If we didn't get those sections off, the force of the current would carry them away. We don't have phone service at the cottage and if we did, who would we call? There was only one person in the area who could maybe get those sections off the frame and up on land and it was me.

I crawled instead of walked to the end of the pier, which was now under water and slippery. There I reached into the water to release the spring clamp that held the wood sections in place and lifted each one off and pulled them along over the remaining sections and carried them to shore. There were eight sections of pier, each about three feet by four feet, forty-five to fifty pounds and wet, slippery and cumbersome.

Charlie was nervously sitting up in the cottage watching, knowing that if I fell in, there was nothing he could do. Why I didn't think to put on a life jacket, I don't know, but I'm not sure I would have had enough free movement to lift the heavy platforms up and off the pier if I was wearing a preserver.

When I finally finished and climbed back up to the cottage, Charlie said he was watching because if the current washed me away he wanted to wave goodbye. He explained that he felt it the decent thing to do since we'd been married for fifty-nine years. He's a caring man!

The trip did perk us up a bit and we had something else to think and talk about for a while. It was an adventure, but we decided that we wouldn't take any more trips to the cottage. With no phones we knew it wasn't the best place to be while Charlie was having problems. So it wasn't long before we were looking for something exciting to do.

My best thinking happens when I'm supposed to be sleeping. Actually, that is up for debate. If there's a problem, I lie awake at night thinking about it. Several ideas for articles I've written were conceived while lying awake at night. So on this night, I was thinking about Charlie's lack of things to do and what to do about it. He was despondent about his condition. He needed some excitement in his life.

Earlier that day, a widowed friend called me. We were bemoaning our ages and things we found either difficult or impossible to do now that we were in our eighties. She mentioned she liked taking baths, but she had difficulty getting out of the tub. I told her that I too had trouble getting out of the tub.

That was what I was thinking about instead of sleeping. Before the night was over, I had the answer to both my husband's and my friend's problem. Charlie was going to have a whole new career. In fact, Charlie was once again going to be president of a company.

I reached for my bedside pen and pad of paper and scribbled information for a business card:

If you are having trouble getting out of the bathtub, call:
UPS-A-DAISY, INC.
All it takes is one good jerk and you're up and on your way.
For a good jerk, call CHARLIE KRUSE, President
Phone #: xxx-xxx-xxx
Wealthy Widows Call Collect

It was a ridiculous premise and where it came from, I don't know, but it worked. The next day Charlie got busy with his computer designing business cards and printing them. As a final touch, he added the following at the bottom of the card: "Wealthy Widows Call Collect." He had a ball handing them out to his friends who were about the same age as he was. The instigator of this idea, my 81-year-old friend, also got a kick out of it. In fact, when we were in Florida, we got a nasty letter from her complaining about Charlie starting a business, getting her interested, and then leaving town. She said she hadn't had a bath for weeks until she found an older man in the area who said he would be happy to help. She took him up on his offer, but it didn't go well. He was tugging and instead of pulling her out of the tub, he fell in. And, hopefully, that is the end of *that* story!

After we spent the season in Florida where Charlie was able to swim every day, he was able to walk and we returned home to Wisconsin without his walker. He will still have to take antibiotics the rest of his life, but as far as his new company, Ups-A-Daisy, Inc., he's thinking of retiring.

The Ups-A-Daisy story is pretty silly, but it's true, and there are true stories out there almost as ridiculous. Here's an example:

Charlie had a doctor's appointment and I went along. We were sitting in the waiting room. A lady and her husband came into the room and sat next to me. She was gazing at her beautiful long, fake fingernails. Suddenly, I heard her say to her husband, "I lost a fingernail!" Pause. "I hope it's not in someone's salad."

There was an even longer pause and then "or maybe it's in the pie!"

At least Ups-A-Daisy, Inc. was just a figment of my imagination. This lady was dead serious.

Chapter 37

Entries in a diary kept at the cottage keeps each family group up-to-date on what is happening, where the fish are biting, whether a deer, porcupine, or bald eagle was sighted, etc. I also write a newsletter, "Up North Up Date," a couple of times a year. This was an article I posted in the newsletter after a trip Charlie and I made to the cottage:

"Just wanted to share some sightings while we were at the cottage this past week. Just a short distance from the cottage we saw a black bear leave the road and run into the woods. Later that evening, while sitting on the porch, we saw that same bear or his friend walk down through the woods to the river. Last trip up we saw "scat" in the road, so I'm sure there is a bear that has taken up residence in the area.

There were huge snapping turtles on the gravel road. Must be egg-laying time.

We also saw a mature and young eagle fly upriver. There were lots of beautiful butterflies everywhere in the woods. This is a butterfly year.

Four deer at different times walked along the riverbank. One was right by the pier. We put a salt block across the river, but they hadn't found it yet.

We also saw a mama duck with fourteen babies. Either she laid lots of eggs or took in an orphaned family. They swam so close behind each other they looked like they were tied together.

While Grandpa and I were playing cards at dusk, we watched a raccoon walking on the pier. He then walked up the path, up the deck steps, the full length of the patio door, looked in at us and sniffed.

I sorted through the kindling and newspapers in the copper boiler by the wood store and found newspapers from 1995. Must have been awhile since that was cleaned. We could use more kindling if anyone has any.

The best news was what we didn't see and that was new leaks in the breezeway since Grandpa resealed the chimney. Maybe we have finally gotten it solved.

To top off our list of sightings, on the way home, as we turned off Highway 13 to get to Highway 8, we saw a bobcat run from the ditch into the woods. That was a first."

The diary, where we record trip experiences, is kept at the cottage. One entry left by our daughter Marie was particularly entertaining. As I said earlier, when our four children were young we would pack the car and a car top carrier with supplies, load up four kids and usually one friend, and a dog. We had enough groceries, clothing, etc. to supply seven people for three or four days. No one wanted to leave the cottage to drive into town for *anything*.

When Marie, husband Steve, three kids, one or two dogs and supplies head north, they take two cars. In spite of that, hardly a day goes by that they don't make a trip into town(some twenty miles from the cottage) for something. This was a posting in the diary after one of Marie's visits:

"Locked both sets of keys in my car. One step forward and five back day! Okay, one step forward and twenty back. Man from Phillips (a small town twenty miles from cottage) made key using my VIN number on vehicle, delivered it. We hadn't eaten yet, 1:00 PM, were going to Oxbo. Kids and I in car, were just leaving cottage, [our golden lab dog] Daisy got fishing lure stuck in her front leg, tried to pull it out with her teeth and hooked her mouth. Drove to Minocqua [35 miles away] to emergency clinic. She's fine. Three-hundred dollar day and no fun."

We've owned the cottage forty plus years. Charlie and I now make the trip alone. It is the vacation spot of choice for Kari and Marie and families. Our oldest son Chuck lives in China and his family is in Missouri so it is not as accessible to them. Steve has his own country home/cottage so he no longer uses the cottage. However, his daughter Angie and family do.

After one of Angie's trips we found examples of two-year-old Leyna's artwork hanging on display. It will be saved in a scrapbook of pictures and craft projects that now hold art from three generations of children. The artwork ranges from very young finger painting and colored marker scribbling to a picture drawn by an adult son. His artistic offering was of champion fisherwoman Grandma floating downriver, arms in the air, crying for someone to save her while poor loser artist son Steve stands on the dock waving goodbye.

One of the latest entries in the diary was by granddaughter Angie:

Thursday the 7ᵗʰ and getting ready to leave today. I'm always sad to say goodbye, but am so thankful for the time spent here with my family. It was some much needed R & R as I'm just finishing up my first trimester with baby number two [Steven Charles]. The next time we're here, depending on when that is, our family may be plus one and I can't wait! As many memories as I have of my childhood here, I'm so excited to make new ones with my own kids. It's the perfect place to teach them about their Uncle Steven [who was killed in an auto accident at age nineteen]and all his favorite things."

Chapter 38

Charlie and I are on our way home from closing up our cottage for another year. As usual, we left with a lot of good memories and, as long as I'm just sitting here, I'm making note of those memorable thoughts so that I can record them when I get home.

Our last trip each year is always a little sad, but it is also always in the fall of the year when the color is so spectacular you can't stay sad for long. Our "ooh"s," "ah"s and "look to the left, look to the right" are redundant, but we can't help ourselves. The color is nonstop in every direction.

While we were at the cottage, we got double the color pleasure because the trees with their reds, yellow, and oranges were mirrored in the river. We could paper a room with the fall photos we've taken over the years, but we'll be able to start on a second room after this trip.

In spring, the birds fill the forest with their songs: "We're back, I've found a nest and would you like to play house with me?" In fall, it is so quiet we can actually hear a leaf float slowly down through the trees to the forest floor. It is so quiet that when a flock of geese flew over, we could hear the flapping of their wings.

Seeing flocks of geese is a rather new experience here in the North Woods. There are lots of geese in Southern Wisconsin where we live, but not in the north. It's only been in the last three or four years that we've seen them.

There have been several other changes in the forty-five years we've had the cottage. We used to hear coyotes howl and owls hoot at night, but rarely hear them now. There were ruffed grouse along the gravel road, but they are now a rarity. They have been replaced by wild turkeys.

This last trip was spectacular in so many ways. Lighting is so important when you are taking photographs and this trip it was perfect. There was full sun every day, shining down on the beautiful fall trees, bringing out the best in their color. Temperatures were in the high sixties at the time of year we have often had snowflakes. Even wildlife cooperated. We saw ruffed grouse as well as turkeys and a huge flock of merganser docks. Busy little red squirrels were running around laying in a food supply for the long, cold winter. But the biggest surprise of all was the appearance of four wood ducks on the river. We hadn't seen wood ducks for some time. Our Creator went all out the day he designed the wood duck and there they were in all their glory.

When the sun went down, it was soon replaced by a full moon. Nighttime in the forest is usually blackout time, but the moon was at its brightest just for us. We could see the tall dark forms of the trees towering over us and the river looked like a silver ribbon running below. The spotlight was on the Flambeau River.

We filled the wood box, emptied the refrigerator, drained the water system, pulled the window shades, turned off the lights, locked the door and walked up the hill to our car; it was the end of another season.

We're both eighty-one years old, but that doesn't stop us from thinking about next year when, instead of the forest being ablaze with color, it will ring with birds singing in another new year. Oh, and don't forget, the first Wednesday after the opening of fishing season, the annual wood tick race, and, please, you must remember to Hammer Tacks, Not Ticks?

Conclusion

The stories you've read have been, for the most part, about our family. The following two incidents are about strangers, but I feel that in some way it must tell something about me, the author. Either I give off an aura of truthfulness and trustworthiness or I have a promising future as a crook. I'll let you be the judge:

There are two possessions a woman would protect with her life, her children and her purse. So how do you explain the following?

On one of our trips to our winter home in Florida, we made a *very* necessary bathroom stop. As I entered the rest stop I could see straight through the building to the truck parking area. Running toward the building was a lady carrying a bundle in her arms. I continued on into the women's restroom to take care of my problem. When I came out of the booth to wash my hands, that same lady was standing there holding a baby wrapped in a tattered, grubby blanket. She looked desperate. Knowing how I felt just seconds ago, I asked her if she would like me to hold her baby while she went to the bathroom. You could see the look of relief in her eyes as she thanked me, handed me the baby and disappeared into a booth.

She must have had time constraints because when she came out of the booth, she quickly washed her hands while thanking me profusely, then wiping her hands on her jeans she took the baby from me and hurried out the exit.

When I went back to the car, I thought about what had just happened. A desperate woman handed someone she had never seen before her baby. It's an old saying, "when you gotta go, you gotta go," but this was carrying it to the extreme.

The second incident, happened at the Veterans Hospital in Fort Meyers, Florida:

It is not a pleasant experience going to a VA hospital. The waiting rooms are always crowded with veterans of different ages and stages of health needs.

Charlie had an appointment and we were waiting to be called. An elderly lady pushing a wheelchair, most likely carrying her husband, entered the room. The first task for a patient after they check in is to go into the small bathroom off the waiting area for a urine sample. The lady was struggling with the cumbersome wheelchair while trying to hold on to a large purse. Seeing her dilemma, I went to her aid and said, "Why don't you let me hold your purse for you?" She gave me her purse! I went back to sit with Charlie and said, "I just stole that lady's purse."

The purse was returned to the grateful stranger, but I got to thinking that I may have missed my calling. Purse snatching is much less time consuming than writing.

I don't know of what value these two incidents have and what they say about me or the people involved, but you have to admit they are both pretty strange, not unlike all the rest of the stories in this rendering of "Hammer Tacks, Not Ticks."

Biography

In 1931, I was born to Walter and Esther Kamrath Amera in Dalton, Wisconsin. Our family lived in the Dalton/Pardeeville area until I was ten. At age six, I attended Stancer School, a one-room schoolhouse. We moved to Madison, Wisconsin where I attended Lapham Grade School and Central High. I have three sisters, Phyllis, Eunice, and Mary and one brother, Chuck. In 1953, I married Charles Kruse in Madison where we lived for many years before moving to Oregon, Wisconsin. We have four children: Chuck, Kari, Steve, and Marie. We also have eleven grandchildren and eight (with another on the way) great-grandchildren. Charlie and I have been married for sixty years and still reside in Oregon, Wisconsin.